Joseph Alexander was t of England. In his early days he was educated in secondary modern schools. He went on to college and university.

From the age of four, he saw what he could only explain at the time as people who were not there.

His whole life has been spent in the service of uniting the spirit world with the human world.

He is a man full of compassion, and all his works are written with great humour and fun. He says that there is nothing mystical or special about himself. Each one of us, as a child of God, has the ability to have the same connections with the unseen world. His famous saying is that "God does not dismiss us, it is we who dismiss God". He says that God is there for the believer and the unbeliever, for the good and the bad, because God's love is unconditional.

The author is a happy, uncomplicated man, who is never happier than when walking the dog and writing books.

By the same author

Born in Heaven
Talking with Spirit

My Life Between Two Worlds

JOSEPH ALEXANDER

Dunollie

First published in 2006 by
Dunollie Limited

UK Distribution Agent:
Crandon Press
PO Box 300
Wells-next-the-Sea
Norfolk
NR23 1WP

www.josephalexander.net

Copyright © Joseph Alexander, 2006

Printed and bound in Great Britain by Biddle's, King's Lynn

The moral right of the author has been asserted.

All rights reserved. Without limiting the rights under copyright reserved above, no part of this publication may be reproduced, stored or introduced into a retrieval system, or transmitted, in any form or by any means (electronic, mechanical, photocopying, recording or otherwise) without the prior written permission of both the copyright owner and the publisher of this book.

A CIP catalogue record for this book is available from the British Library.

ISBN 0 9548526 1 3

To Casper and Oscar, my magnificent animal friends – honourable and pure

Contents

Very Young	1
Time to Go to School	11
Titus	31
Paul	34
The Valley of the Animals	42
A Teenager Now	45
Obligation	50
Everything Has Energy	52
Making Ends Meet	56
Chou-Li	61
The Spiritualist Church	65
Go North	71
My Other Grandmother	77
The Churchyard	81
Developing a Personal Relationship with God	84
Nobody There	87
My Brother's Car	89
The New House	92
She is Safe and Sound	97
Animals	99
The White Season	102
Spirit Children	105
What Am I Doing Here?	108
Back to School	112
A Haunting	128
Rescued	132
The Rollright Stones	135
With the World in Her Hands	141
The Voice and the People	143

Very Young

One of my earliest memories is of when I was about four years old. I was playing in my bedroom at home, when I noticed that someone was entering the room. I just thought it would be my mum, but when I looked up, to my surprise, I saw a lady I didn't know. She smiled at me. A bright light was shining all around her, and I will never forget the way she spoke: she had a very gentle voice, but to me she sounded like she was talking through a cardboard tube. As children we used to get old cardboard tubes from the carpet shops. Once upon a time the tubes had carried rolled-up carpets, but we made some alterations to them and used them as trumpets so we could play at being soldiers, and her voice reminded me of that.

I had no fear of this lady; in fact I was absolutely

2 Very Young

intrigued by her. I wondered how she could shine the way she did. The scene reminded me of those Christmas plays where there is a fairy princess standing in the middle of the stage with all the lights shining on her.

The lady said to me, "Soon you are going to move house, but Daddy won't be going with you."

I don't remember being upset on hearing that news. I was much more interested in the lady's beauty, which even at the tender age of four enraptured me.

I had never seen clothes like the ones this lady was wearing, and even to this day I can't really say how she was dressed. The nearest I can describe it is to say that her clothes sparkled with colours that were bright but not brassy. As I say, she reminded me of the princess in the Christmas plays put on by my church.

To me this lady was as solid as the bedroom furniture. I have often wondered if she appeared to me in the way she did so that she wouldn't frighten me. If so, it worked.

I seem to recall the lady was about as old as my mum… when you're four, everyone seems old. Please excuse me when I say she was far prettier than my mum. Perhaps it was the colourful clothes she wore and the lights that shone all around her that gave me a biased view.

All these years later I still remember how fascinated I was by everything about this lady, and it still seems like it was only yesterday that she visited. I always feel happy when I think back to that day, and the words she spoke have always stayed with me.

In the innocence of childhood, it never occurred to me that this was not a normal situation to be in.

Mum came into my room to ask who I was talking to. I turned round to answer her; I was going to show her where the lady was standing. But I was in for another surprise, because now the lady had disappeared. I ran to the big cupboard and looked inside. I looked all over the room for her, even under the bed. Mum asked me what I was doing, and who the lady was. I had no idea, though, so I couldn't really tell her much. All I could do was repeat to Mum what the lady had said to me. Mum told me I was a "silly b***er", amongst other things. All her life, even into old age, if Mum was put out, she would never fail to say "You silly b***er!" plus whatever other expletives seemed to fit the occasion.

At this point let me tell you a bit about my mother. Mum had been born into circumstances that were very different from those she found herself in by the time I came along. As a young woman, she was accustomed to luxury. Although by some of today's standards she may not appear to have lived a lavish life, she had certainly come from a well-to-do background. In those days it was considered a disgrace to marry below your own social class – as if money makes a person any better – and her family recoiled at the thought that she had married "down". Mum ended up being disowned by her whole family except Nan (my grandmother). In the circumstances, I'm amazed that Mum coped as well as she did – with the poverty, and everything else that went with it.

In her old age, Nan came to live with Mum and us kids. I felt sorry for her, because I realised what a shock moving into such a poor neighbourhood must have been for a gentle and refined lady like my grandmother.

Many years later I asked Mum about the day that the lady with the light around her appeared in my bedroom. This is what she said to me:

"When you were a baby in the cot, I sometimes felt I didn't want to come near you, because you would be busy laughing and giggling, as though someone was playing games with you. You would throw out your arms as if you were expecting someone to pick you up. And as a toddler, too," she continued, "you would sit down and play as if there was someone there playing with you. You would react just as if one of your brothers or sisters was there, even when they weren't around. To be honest, it was spooky, and I would leave the room. I never felt at ease with you, because you always seemed to be somewhere else. You only seemed to be happy when you were talking to people who weren't there. That time in your bedroom," said Mother, "when you said you'd been talking to that lady, I had a strange feeling of being watched. You made my blood run cold when you said about your dad not moving to the new house with us, because even though you and the rest of the family had no idea, preparations were already well underway for me to move to a new house."

Mum also confirmed that the divorce had gone through about six months after my visitation.

Anyway – back to my story – we soon moved to a new house. All our goods and chattels were put on a handcart. My brother, my sister and I climbed on too and dangled our legs over the side of the cart, thinking what a great adventure we were having. Those were the days when a car was only for the rich, and we were right at the other end of the scale, being very, very poor.

The new house was in a cul-de-sac, on one of those old-fashioned council estates. It had three large bedrooms, a sitting room and a great big kitchen. Over the years the kitchen became the hub of the house. There was a big back garden, too, that was overgrown with grass and weeds.

The next-door neighbours had a beautiful garden. Roses ran from one end of it to the other, and some of them hung over into our garden too. Sometimes my brothers and sisters and I would pick the roses and take them upstairs to make our bedrooms look pretty. Other times we would make scent out of the rose petals.

In the new house I was to have more strange experiences, the first of which took place as soon as I stepped through the front door. When you came into our new house, the first thing you would see was the staircase. I came through the door, looked up, and saw a little girl standing on the stairs, just one step below the landing. I was wondering what she could be doing here, when she spoke to me.

"My name's Lalla," she said. "And I'm going to be your friend!"

I asked her where she lived, but she just laughed at me.

"Here, silly! With you now!" she said.

"You can't," I replied. "Mummy won't allow it. Anyway, we haven't got enough money to have somebody else living here with us."

Once we had finished moving in and things had settled down a little, I told Mum about the little girl called Lalla. To this day I remember her reaction:

"You're a (many expletives deleted) silly, silly boy! Now you stop this nonsense at once or I'll smack your a***!"

She might as well have done, so hard was she shaking me. In those days that was Mum's answer to everything we did that annoyed her. She wouldn't smack us, she would shake us instead. Mum was a powerful woman. Today we would say she was big-boned, but back then we used to say she was covered with oodles of meat, and it was meat that could easily shake a small boy off his feet. If we kids were slow to guess what she wanted, or how annoyed she was, she would make sure we found out PDQ by shaking some sense into us.

Life soon settled down. My brothers and sisters started at their new school, but I was not yet of school age. I was left at home a lot of the time on my own, but I didn't mind at all because I had my unseen friends to play with. It was about this time that a new friend joined me. He was a big boy of six. He told me his name was Ralph, but I called him Rally. He said he had lived in a place called Italy, which of course meant nothing to me at the time.

People had told me it was weird to talk about friends that no one else could see. But my friends were real, and they were perfectly normal. It was only other people who thought they were strange. I could see them, hear them, talk to them and play with them, and the biggest problem for me was trying to work out why other people couldn't. I always thought it was very odd that Mum forbade me to speak about them. Eventually I became completely disheartened about mentioning my unseen friends to anyone. No one seemed to understand, and I knew there was a good chance I'd have the living daylights shaken out of me.

I did get very scared one day, though, when Rally told me that he was dead. He said that he was a spirit. I remember thinking that being dead sounded like a bad thing. But I couldn't quite work it out. To my mind, dead people were ghosts who lived in graveyards. My unseen friends weren't like that at all – they were real people, just like me. They certainly weren't dead.

One day I asked Lalla if it was really true that Rally was a dead boy, and she said, "Of course he is, silly! And so am I! I'm a spirit too!"

There had been times when I had thought my friends were different from me in some ways, but I had no idea they were dead. I wanted to tell Mum what Lalla had said, but it didn't seem like a good idea.

By the time I was older, it was easier for me to see why people had been frightened of me…

As the years passed, I often wondered why Mum had not told me there and then that the people I spoke to were dead. One day I managed to get her onto the subject. Mum said that in those days it was considered a weakness to have a child that was different from the rest. She said that because we had just moved into a new neighbourhood, she didn't want people thinking that she had a lunatic child. She also told me she was afraid the neighbours would point at her and talk about her behind her back every time she went out of the house. She went on to say that since my brothers and sisters were at school and I had no one to play with, she thought I had invented imaginary friends. And she said she hoped that by moving to a new house all this nonsense about seeing people who were not there would stop.

I am convinced that Mum knew I was telling the truth about my unseen friends, and it frightened her.

Time to Go to School

The next time something funny happened was just after I had started going to school. I was walking home one day when I was stopped in the street by a very elderly couple. The old man said his name was Jack. The old lady who was with him was his wife, and she was called Maude. She was very stooped.

"I live next door to you," said Jack.

I knew he didn't, because my friends did, but he smiled at me, and said, "Yes, I do live there, but in a different way now."

Then a friend of Mum's came along the street and asked me who I was talking to. I turned to show her the couple, but they must have walked on, and Mum's friend didn't see them. Mum's friend walked the rest of the way home with me, and she came into the house. She told Mum exactly what she had seen.

12   Time to Go to School

I knew I was in for big trouble.

That afternoon I got more than just a shaking, I can tell you. I got no tea or supper, and I was locked inside my bedroom. I was so upset because I knew I was telling the truth. Why was I being punished? It wasn't my fault that Mum's friend didn't see the old couple. How could she have missed them when they were standing there, as plain as day?

Some weeks later Mum called me into our sitting room. She had two of her other friends with her. Mum asked me to recount what I had seen on my way home from school that day.

Why should I do that, I thought. It would only mean I would be in trouble again and I would get locked in my bedroom. (All my life since, I have hated having my bedroom door closed…) Or I might get a good shaking. I hesitated to say anything at all, but Mum told me I would get my bottom smacked if I didn't answer the question. Grown-ups are so strange sometimes!

Anyway, I told my story to Mum's friends. One of them asked me to describe Jack. I told her that he had a funny foot with a big shoe on it, and he was a cobbler by trade.

One of Mum's friends said that Jack and Maude

had lived next door to our house, and Jack had been a cobbler. They had both been dead for about twenty years, and Jack had had something called a club foot.

"Tell us about your other friends, then," said Mum.

I was worried I was going to get shaken yet again. But one of Mum's friends said to her, "You know, you have a gifted child."

I remember thinking that nobody had given me any gifts! It was all very strange to me.

This was one of the very few times in my childhood when not only did I see my mum looking like the cat that had stolen the cream, but also I was allowed to stay and talk to her friends about unseen people.

Like most children of that age, I got pretty absorbed in the life that was going on around me. Collecting and trading marbles and cigarette cards were my greatest sources of pleasure, closely followed by playing at being soldiers. But my strange experiences with the spirit world continued.

One time, when I was six, I went pop-bottling around the neighbours' houses. In those days you got a penny for every pop bottle you returned, and a halfpenny for every jam jar. It was a good way for us kids to earn some pocket money. I had decided to go to some houses that were quite far away from where I lived, because this gave me a better chance that the other kids wouldn't have been there already.

I was heading for the front door of one particular house when I was met by an elderly man. He didn't speak to me, and I didn't say a word either, because I was so astonished by the way he looked. He was wearing an old-fashioned military uniform. With hindsight and age, I now realise he was dressed as a redcoat.

"Are you going to a fancy dress party?" I asked him.

I can only say he scowled at me.

"I am a soldier," he pronounced.

But he didn't look like any of the soldiers I knew about. I remember thinking that if anyone should know whether he was a soldier or not, I should. After all, at six years of age playing soldiers was one of my main occupations. I certainly didn't get any pop bottles from him, and to this day I have no idea why I saw him.

Another time I was sitting on a wall at the end of our cul-de-sac, when a group of monks came walking towards me. At that stage I had no idea these people were called monks – I only found out when I was older. Anyway, one of them stopped and spoke to me.

"This is holy land. You are trespassers here!"

This was just gobbledegook to me. I didn't really understand what he meant by "holy land", and I had even less idea what a trespasser was.

I couldn't tell Mum what had happened because I knew how much trouble I would be in. Instead I told my priest at Sunday school, but he just said I should forget about it.

Years later Mum told me that the priest had in fact come to see her about the matter – even though at the time I had tried hard not to involve her. Apparently he asked Mum whether before the day I saw the monks she had ever mentioned to me that there was supposed to have been a monastery nearby, back in the days when the land in question had been farmed.

I must say that I never tried to find out whether the theory about there being a monastery in the area was actually true. I was quite squeamish about the whole matter, and in fact I still am, because of the sense of unease that I got from the monks. The monk that spoke was definitely unfriendly, and the event has no relevance to my life. I say let sleeping dogs lie.

16   Time to Go to School

My early school years were a mixed bag of sweets, really. My friends were all kids who only knew me from school, and I was happy with their comradeship. The children from around where I lived avoided me like the plague – there was no way they were going to be associated with "that weird kid".

I didn't relate well to my brothers and sisters, nor they to me – either at home or at school – because they considered me an oddball. I was a source of embarrassment to them, and they tried their very best to distance themselves from me. Of course now I can see it from their point of view – who wants a brother that talks into thin air to people you can't see? I suppose in a way it was my own fault that neighbours would forbid their children to play with me, and adults would cross to the other side of the road when they saw me coming...

In my first few years at school I was lucky enough to have a really lovely lady as my headmistress. Many people thought of her as eccentric, including some of her staff, but this suited me just fine, because at lunchtimes she liked me to come into her office where she would listen to me talk about my unseen friends. We decided that the things we talked about would be our little secret, although I'm sure the staff must have guessed. It was a bonus for me, because it meant I didn't have to sit in the dining room having other kids make fun of me.

One of the things my headmistress was most interested in was to hear what I thought about life after death. I can see myself now, sitting in her office feeling very important, with my legs swinging because my feet didn't touch the floor, and telling her what came into my head. And I can still see her sweet face, listening to me as if I was some clever professor giving a speech on the theory of relativity.

I still have the same views about life after death today as I did then; the only difference is that now I have a deeper understanding of the subject.

At one stage I got the measles, and this kind lady came around to our house and brought me my school dinner on a plate. School dinners were free dinners for families like ours, and she didn't want me to miss out on a meal. We remained great friends right up until she died when I was in my twenties.

Near to where I lived as a child there were some blackberry bushes. I often used to go there, and I would spend many a happy hour gathering blackberries. A little further on there was a bluebell wood. This was the special place I used to go to on my own.

Time to Go to School

I would walk, pick bluebells, sit under the trees feeling happy and contented, and listen to music that no one else could hear. Walking home with as many bluebells as I could carry, as many jam jars stuffed with blackberries as I could fit in my hands, and a face covered in blackberry juice, I must have looked a right little ragamuffin. It was from these days that my never-ending love of music began.

At the time I had an "unseen" friend called Robert who used to come and teach me about music. Robert taught me how to lose myself in music when times were bad. Since I was often in trouble, I found his advice very useful.

A lot of the trouble was of my own making, because I didn't grasp the importance of being tactful and diplomatic. To be quite honest, perhaps I was egotistical. I was a crass youngster, but in a naive way. My brother was far more sophisticated than I was, with a natural charm that endeared him to people. It may have been helpful to me – and to my spirit friends, for that matter – if one of the things they had taught me was how to be charming. I could have done with learning when it was fine to speak and when it was better not to. The ironic thing is that by the time I was in my teens, people said that

I was the charming one, and my brother was the handsome one… which indeed he was. There's no getting away from the fact, though, that as a child I was very sensitive. Or as my family would have put it, in the dialect, I was a "mardy-ar**d little bu**er".

Often I felt resentful at being different from the other kids. When you are young, you want to be one of the gang, and I certainly wanted to. Instead I ended up going off and listening to a whole lot of music that no one else could hear! I guess there was a part of me that wanted to escape the crowd, too.

One day during one of my walks, Robert came to me. He was looking very sad, so I asked him what was wrong. He said that when he was on earth he had died in a fire, and he had not had time to grow up, so he was about to come back and be born in a place called Somalia. The problem was that Robert had been living with his grandparents, and he didn't want to leave them, or me.

I understood the words Robert was saying, but I didn't really know what he meant by "coming back". I remember thinking that if he was living with his grandparents now, and he didn't want to leave me, why would he have to come back..? As a child I was not the brightest button in the box; my brother was the brains of the family. Even so, from the way Robert was talking about coming back, I could tell it was something serious.

After that day I never saw Robert again. I missed him, and it really saddened me.

A few months after Robert had gone, I was playing in our garden with a friend called Alan. Alan was a real boy, made of flesh and blood. Oh! How many people do you know who need to explain that some of their friends are made of flesh and blood..!? Anyway, Alan and I were playing one of our favourite games. We were making mud pies, then throwing them and seeing if they would hit the washing line. We were quite absorbed in doing this, when I became aware of a little girl standing by our garden shed. I was surprised to see her. I have already told you I was not quick on the uptake: having already seen many souls from the spirit world, you would think I would be used to them. But they still always startled me – each time that one appeared seemed like the first time I had ever seen one. The little girl smiled at me.

"My name's Maureen," she said. "Can I play with you?"

"Yes," I said.

My friend Alan looked at me and realised I was off

on one of my funnies again. Suddenly he yelled out: "Bloody hell! I can see a girl by the shed!"

Bloody… great! I thought. There's another one like me!

I never told this story to anyone, from that day to this, to protect Alan. Having one oddball in the neighbourhood was enough. Alan and I are still friends, even now. And Maureen has been a lifelong friend to me too; she is still my personal confidante.

Some time later I had a terribly sad day when my little dog, Floss, died. I was heartbroken. He was my mate and my world. In my mind's eye I can still see those intense little eyes staring up at me, trying to make sense of what I was saying to him. Out of all the people in my world, Floss was the one I really loved – to me he was a person. He would listen to me, and he knew more about me than anyone in the world. Today, as I write about him, I am sitting here crying.

One day Floss came back to me. I heard a bark; it was a kind of bark that I had only ever heard Floss make, and usually only when he was excited. I looked up and saw him racing across the garden towards me with his tail wagging. He leapt up into my arms, and licked me all over my face.

22   Time to Go to School

Maureen told me that Floss was never far from me. She said that I had been asleep when Floss came back. But the dream I had been having was one of those ones that are absolutely real – I felt no different than if I had been wide awake.

At times I have known great happiness in my life, but I can tell you that seeing Floss again – even though it was in a dream – was the purest happiness I have ever felt. I can still feel the joy of that moment; I am that little boy again.

Those childhood days seem far-off now, but there are plenty of details that stay with you forever.

I remember the time when my need for a pair of sports shoes for school taught me a harsh lesson. The day when we had PE was approaching fast, and the closer it got, the more desperate I felt. I knew that if I didn't have any, I would be humiliated in front of my whole class. The teacher would tell me I couldn't take part, I would have to go off and sit in a corner, and the whole class would laugh at me for being the only one without the right shoes.

To my shame, I went round to the local shoe shop and blurted out, "Mum said could you please let me have a pair of sports shoes until her pay day." How I had the nerve to ask, I have no idea, as I was a timid child at the best of times. But it worked, and I got my shoes. I hadn't thought about the reckoning with Mum, though. When she asked me where I'd got them, I lied shamelessly, telling her I'd been tidying up people's gardens and had saved up the money.

After the PE lesson I felt really wicked about having lied. I was frightened that God would punish me by telling Mum and the shopkeeper what had really happened. On top of this, my spirit friends had told me it was always best to tell the truth, so I felt absolutely dreadful, and I took myself to the shoe shop and sobbed out the truth.

Luckily the shopkeeper forgave me. He said he wouldn't tell Mum this time, but I must never lie to him again. I guess he must have felt sorry for me, because once the talking was over, he gave me a three-penny piece. In a way I did get punished, though, because Mum said that if I could tidy other people's gardens, I could tidy ours too.

On a happier note, I got a nice surprise one day at Sunday school. Every now and then the teachers would give us Bible quizzes. I wasn't much of a reader at that age, but one day it seemed like I must have been reading the Bible from cover to cover, and I won the quiz. I was given two prizes. One was a miniature version of the Bible, and the other was a picture of Christ, called *Behold, I Stand at the Door and Knock.* At the time I didn't think my spirit friends had given me any help to win the quiz. I didn't see them and I didn't hear them. But somehow, on that particular day, all the right answers just kept popping into my head…

One person I will never forget was the old man who lived in our street. He had a bad leg, but he still used to ride his bike all over town. One day, when I was about ten, I was standing by our front gate just as he was walking by. At that moment, everything around me appeared to change. I felt like I had been at the dentist's and been given laughing gas. I was still aware of my surroundings, but I felt disoriented and unreal. The air was shimmering, the way it does above a flame. It looked to me like I was at a crossroads. The old man was there too, standing by his bike. Just as he started moving off, a lorry came down the hill and hit him and his bike; they both went under the wheels. I got such a shock that I screamed out loud. Then everything came back into focus.

I was shaking, and wondering if what I had seen had really happened. The old man was still outside our gate. He had stopped, and now he was standing right in front of me and asking what was wrong. Being young and naive, I just blurted everything out to him.

"Oh, don't worry," he said.

I could tell by the look in his eyes that he felt sorry for me, obviously thinking to himself that it was that daft kid again. As he walked away, I heard a voice say to me, "I'm Elsie, his wife. Would you please pass a message to my husband?"

So I called out to the old man, telling him that Elsie had a message for him. He came back to me, but by now his cheeks were flushing with anger.

"How do you know my wife's name?" he snapped.

I told him what I had heard.

"You're a stupid little bugger", he told me.

I was so shocked that I just burst into tears. I was left standing at our front gate with this old man glaring at me. It was a very upsetting day.

A year or so later the old man was killed by a lorry outside the factory where he worked. He had been at the crossroads, crossing the road.

Some years later I went to the wedding of one of his sons, and I saw the old man standing in the church, at the side of the altar. He nodded to me.

I liked to think that in that nod, he was sort of thanking me. But that was probably just me wanting to prove to him that I had been right – the egotistical little monkey that I was.

To any bright child, self-preservation would have seemed like a very good idea. I should have learned to stop and think, and maybe to keep my mouth shut. Goodness knows, I'd been told enough times. But no… I kept charging in like a bull in a china shop.

Really I was very naughty, because I had been expressly forbidden to talk about my unseen friends to anyone.

My indiscretions were now causing great embarrassment to my family. I wasn't endearing myself to my brothers and sisters, but it was worse for my mother, as she was in the unenviable position of feeling she had to defend me to outsiders. Poor Mum would be walking on eggshells whenever her friends came round to the house, in case I opened my mouth and the words "I have a message for you" came out again. I was doing myself no favours, and I ended up being banned from the house whenever we had visitors.

None of this stopped me from sneaking around to the neighbours' houses and telling them about the "unseen" friends that were there with them. Many a cake and sticky bun came my way as a reward. But this careless talk caused me a lot of trouble, too. There were times when news got back to Mum, and then I really copped it.

With the benefit of hindsight, I can't help wondering if I was indulging myself a little. It occurs to me now that I might have been getting a thrill out of being able to pass on messages to people, and I suspect I was a little too fond of the sweets and cakes that were coming my way.

People who work in this field will tell you this: There is far more to it than just being in contact with Spirit and passing on messages. For a start, the people you speak to, whether seen or unseen, have their own feelings and personalities. So when a soul comes and asks for his or her message to be passed on to an earthly person, it means, at the very least, that he or she has had the caring and made the time and the effort to come. Just as you would with any earthly person who speaks to you, you treat the soul in the spirit world with respect, giving them the time to air whatever they need to discuss. One major thing that I hadn't learned at all as a child was tact!

Eventually I started to feel more comfortable

Time to Go to School

dealing with different people in different situations. And as the years passed and I grew more mature, I became more and more aware of my responsibility both towards those in the spirit world and those I met in this world.

At the same time, though, I wasn't very pleased with the psychic and spiritual things that were going on in my life. My feeling was why should all this be happening to me. To be honest, I didn't want it to happen. I wanted to be the same as all the rest of the kids. It was a close-knit community that I lived in, and I so much wanted to be a part of everything that was going on. This was definitely a complicated time for me. I didn't have the intellectual power to sort out my feelings and define what I needed. On the other hand, I knew deep inside that the people I was seeing and the talks I was having with Spirit were a reality. Then on top of that, I often got the feeling when I talked to other people that they thought I was two sandwiches short of a picnic.

I will tell you about a spirit that came to me one night; it was the first time that a spirit had got me really frightened.

Everyone was in bed asleep, but I had woken up because I needed to go to the toilet. As was common in those days, the toilet was outside the house. Ours was beside the back door. So I got out of bed and walked downstairs, and then outside. Just as I was coming out of the toilet and about to go back inside, I saw a man sitting on the wall. He was only about two feet away from the toilet door, and I felt scared by the way he seemed to be glaring at me; in my mind's eye I can still see his face even today. He had a huge black beard that went down to his chest, and a strange hat on his head. I thought it was a bit like a bishop's hat, only not as fancy. He spoke in a strange tone of voice that I could hardly understand.

Then he told me that I sat in the Sanhedrin. I was a young boy at the time, and for all that I could understand, he might as well have been telling me that I came from Mars. He frightened me, and even now his words send chills through me. I just gave him one of my blank looks.

"Young man!" he thundered. "Do not do as I did and put perjuries in your way! Believe what you see and hear."

I struggled for days to make any sense of his words, and for a long time afterwards I was afraid of going to the toilet at night on my own.

Looking back over what I have written, it must

seem like my childhood was one big long misery, but actually that is far from true. In *My Personal Journey* I write about the wonderful characters I have met in my life, and the funny situations I have found myself in. It has been a tremendous life, with so much fun and laughter. You see it is not only the saints who put a twinkle in God's eye – it is ordinary people like you and me, too.

Titus

When I was about eleven I had one of the most vivid experiences of my childhood. Even now when I think back to it, after so many years have passed, I still have that same sense of dread mixed in with excitement.

In those days I shared a bedroom with my brother. I had gone to bed early that night, but I had a throbbing toothache, and I was still wide awake.

Suddenly the room seemed to fill with light. I thought my brother had come in and turned the light on. I was about to bellow at him to turn it off, but as I turned and looked towards the door, I was stunned to see a very tall man standing at the end of the bed.

"Mum! Come quick!" I screamed at the top of my voice. "There's a man in my room!"

Titus

Mum came rushing up the stairs and into the room, and switched on the light. I was trembling all over.

"Oh, you've had a nightmare, you silly boy."

Why couldn't Mum see the man? He was still standing there! He was as clear as day! But she just gave her usual answer to anything that irritated her.

"You silly b***er! You behave, or you'll get the back of my hand around your ear!"

She switched the light off, left the room and shut the door behind her. But the room was still bathed in light, and I was left with this man still standing at the end of the bed. He smiled, and spoke to me:

"Do not be afraid, for I come in the name of the Father. He has heard your prayers and seen your tears. The truth of all you see of the divine world will one day come to the realisation of your world. And soon a visitor will come to you, who will walk with you throughout your life."

Then the light began to fade, and the man with it. As he went, he said, "My name is Titus."

The next thing I knew it was morning, and to my great shame I had wet the bed, something I hadn't done since I was a much younger child. My brother was none too pleased, and before long all the family and quite a few of my friends knew about it – to my horror. Children can certainly be cruel...

I felt ill for days after the visit from this man. In fact I always feel upset when I see a spirit bathed in light, even to this day, although I have very little reaction when a spirit comes that isn't bathed in light. As time passed, I realised that I don't believe I'm good enough to see the spirits that are bathed in light. Somewhere within me I feel that if a spirit is bathed in light, then he or she has risen to a Godlike state of awareness, and this makes me acutely aware of my own fragilities.

In any case, there was no way I wanted to go back into the bedroom that I had been sharing with my brother. I had developed a fear of seeing that man again. But I suppose I had a natural resilience, like all children, and within a few weeks I was back to being myself. Thank goodness there was no more bed-wetting. Well, not for a while, at least.

All I can remember from the next little while is that I started spending more and more time with my spirit friends and going for walks in the park and the woods. It was so different back in those days – you never had a fear of being attacked, like the youth of today have. Maybe I was just lucky.

Paul

It had become a way of life in my family by now that on Saturdays we would all do our own thing. Mum would go and catch the latest films with her friends. My sisters, as often as not, would go up to the local park to play with their friends and meet up with the boys. And my brothers would go out playing with their seemingly hundreds of mates. But I, being so young, had to be back in the house by seven on the dot. Looking back, I realise what a slow boy I must have been, because it never occurred to me to stay out later. If I had done, my family would certainly never have noticed…

So Saturday nights would see me sitting in the kitchen by the fire, listening to the radio and snuggling down into one of the big old armchairs. We had two armchairs – one on either side of the fire – and a big old kitchen table up against the back wall. I hated that table, because it was my job to scrub it with carbolic soap, baking soda, and a hard brush. But I loved our old valve radio, and I loved my Saturday nights. The kitchen was the hub of the house in those days, and on Saturday night it was my kingdom. I used to put extra lumps of coal on the fire and brew myself a pot of tea. Then I would slice up some bread and pile on the jam.

One Saturday night I was listening to the wireless, as we used to call it then, and looking into the fire, as usual, but suddenly I started to get an eerie feeling. I realised that someone had come into the room, and the thought covered me in goose pimples. I was too frightened to look around, but eventually I forced myself. Standing by the pantry door was a man of medium build, with quite a small face. His eyes really held me; they were so piercing, and they never left my eyes the whole time he was there.

To this day I remain ashamed of what I did next. I grabbed a fork that had been lying on the table, and I threw it at him with all my might. But it passed straight through his body and stuck into the panel of the door. He gave not the slightest reaction. And I couldn't understand how the fork hadn't hurt him.

36   Paul

If you threw something like a fork at a human, it would definitely hurt them... To me, he was as real and as solid as I was. I hadn't realised in my young mind that you can't hurt a spirit.

I guess to have thrown something that hard I really must have been in a state of terror. But if I was terrified then, I felt even worse when he started to move closer to me. This man walked around the table, heading for the armchair opposite mine.

I started to notice more details about his appearance. His hair was quite fair, and a lock of it fell forward over his face. In later years I came to know this as a kiss curl; someone famous in the fifties had one, and when I saw it, I thought back to this night.

He came and sat down opposite me. I was sitting so far back in my chair that it was pressed hard up against the wall behind me. Still he had not taken his eyes off me. Once again, I'm ashamed to say, I wet myself. But at the time there were just so many different terrors running through me that my sense of shame was the last thing I was thinking about. Part of the reason I felt so awful was that I had absolutely no idea what was happening. I thought I must be in the presence of something very bad indeed. All I wanted was to do was run – far away from this man.

Up until now he had not spoken to me. When he did, his voice was quiet and gentle, but very deep.

"Do not be afraid," he said. "I am the one that Titus spoke of to you. I am Paul, and you will find me in the Great Book of Life."

At the time these words meant nothing to me. What did register with me was my mounting sense of horror. I was remembering how the minister at my church had told me that if I didn't stop talking about dead people the way I did, a devil would come and take me away and I would burn in hell forever.

Paul laughed and said, "I am no devil. I am of God the Father."

It was only later that I realised he had read my mind. I certainly hadn't uttered a word to him; I was almost too scared to breathe. But I was still consumed by the thought that this man must be a devil. I shot forward in my chair, ready to dash out of the room. But as I did, Paul caught hold of my hand and gently sat me back down in the chair. His hands were very strong, and very real.

The intensity of the feeling I had that night has never left me, even all these years later. What I experienced was a feeling of unreality, and at the same time, a strong sense of knowing that all this was really happening. Although it sounds contradictory, that is the best that I can describe it. Maybe it was my deep sense of shock that caused this feeling, or maybe it was something that Paul did to help allay my fears.

Paul then began talking to me. But I found what he said so strange that a couple of times I even burst out laughing. Somehow it was easy to laugh when I was feeling so scared. Most of what he said went way over my head. In fact to my child's mind it sounded ridiculous. Even the bits that I *could* understand didn't seem like they could be real. He spoke at length about future events, but they made no sense to me. I was in such a state that there was no way I could think sensibly about anything, and I was certainly too young to take in anything intellectual.

Paul did say he would walk with me throughout my life, and that many others would too. I couldn't really understand that at the time, either, but much time has passed now, and I can see how very true these words were.

Paul went on to say I would know great sadness and suffering. I just remember thinking that if he had really come from God, surely he must have known how much I had suffered already… I really felt hard done by! And I was ever ready to play the martyr. But when I think about it now, I realise that thousands of kids across the world would have given their right arm to be in my position and to have what I had. Paul also said I would know great happiness and joy in my life, and this has turned out to be true, too.

Then while I was sitting there with Paul, something happened that was to shape my life forever. I suddenly realised I was standing in a garden. There was an arch nearby, the sort that people grow roses around, which I walked through. But I was surprised, because it was not just an ordinary arch; it was also a kind of gateway. On the other side stood a monk. He was very plump and had a huge fleshy smile, and in my youthful estimation, he looked just like Friar Tuck…

A moment later I found myself in a different garden. I was now standing in front of a building unlike any I had ever seen. It was big and beautiful, and it had windows that reminded me of the stained glass we see in our cathedrals. But what fascinated me the most was that as I stood there looking at this building, its walls kept changing colour. And not only were they changing colour, but they also seemed to be moving and vibrating. My logical mind couldn't make head or tail of what was happening, but I felt so happy and exuberant that I started dashing towards the building anyway. But the monk stepped forward and stopped me. He told me that I was still an earth child, and I was being shown a time to come.

Then he led me back to the gateway and through the arch. As I left, the monk pressed something into my hand, and I clenched my fist tight. The next thing I knew I was back in the kitchen, in the armchair, with Paul asking me if I had enjoyed my journey.

I still remember opening my clenched fist to see what I had been given, and finding to my disappointment that there was nothing there. Paul told me I had been given the key to something. As to what it is, though, your guess would be as good as mine. All these years later it's still a mystery to me, but I'll wait and see… I've learned patience.

In time I came to understand that I had astral travelled that night; in other words I had left my physical body.

As the years passed, I went on to have many visions of future events. Each vision has subsequently turned to historical fact, and many have been of major national and international significance.

Paul told me that night to remember my dreams,

saying that many years down the road they would play an important part in other people's lives. Well, I am of mature years now, and I have to say that so far I don't think they've been important to anyone in particular that I know of. But like my visions, my dreams have been meaningful in a general way, signalling events before they have happened.

I have no intention yet of packing my suitcases to move into the spirit world; hopefully I have a long time to go. But after my journey that night, I lost all fear of the afterlife. I still get jumpy, though, if I see a spirit person I don't recognise! Silly, isn't it…

Paul proved to be a great help to my life in many ways. He taught me how to concentrate, and how to behave like a good and responsible student (well, as far as that was possible in my case). Paul showed me that I could avoid trouble at school by not talking to my pals about Spirit the whole time, and by refraining from interrupting the teacher.

I never told my family anything about Paul's visit until years later, when I was far too old to be rebuked.

The Valley of the Animals

I have had the honour of visiting places in the spirit world that are magical beyond description, and many of these journeys have helped to shape the rest of my life.

Some time after Paul's visit, I had a dream that I was travelling on a very long road. I knew I was asleep, but it felt like I was awake. I was astral travelling again. After what seemed like a few moments I met a young lady at the side of the road, and she spoke to me. I didn't feel afraid, and neither did I feel like I was in a world that was in any way strange to me – it all seemed completely natural. The young lady took me by the hand, and the next thing I knew, I realised I was flying with her. How this was happening, I still don't know to this day, but soon I found myself in a very steep valley.

This was a valley of splendour and grace. The grasses and trees were coloured in the most brilliant and natural greens, and indeed the colours were breathtaking everywhere. Rivers wended their way through the valley, and gloriously coloured birds flew overhead. Peace and beauty filled my senses. I was truly amazed.

"Where am I? Where is this place?" I asked the young lady.

"It is a part of the Valley of the Animals," she said. "This is where the animals come to live in peace and serenity."

I asked her whether animals have souls.

"Every creature that God creates has a soul, in some way or another," she replied. "That is why it is so important that you respect all life for what it is, and for what it means to your world. Some forms of life, such as mankind, were created to be higher beings, and are entrusted to be the caretaker of all of God's creations. Other forms of life were created to be magnificent animals, with great intelligence and great understanding of the Earth. I have brought you here so you will learn that the animals of your world are the respecters of your world. Stop, look, and listen, and you will learn much from them."

Seeing the tiger and the lamb walking side by side remains one of my most vivid memories. A powerful feeling of harmony and love came from these two creatures.

"I will always remember the peace and serenity that I have seen today, and how kind you have been in bringing me here," I told the young lady.

All my life I have felt humbled by this experience.

It is a great comfort to know that when our beloved pets fall asleep, they live on, just as we do, and they are cared for, just as we are.

I have visited the Valley of the Animals many times over the years. Some of the visits I have made have really sustained me in times when I otherwise might have felt very down, or unwell. I even find it uplifting just to lie down and recall these visits in my conscious mind. All my life I have dearly loved animals. I became a vegan because I could not bear to think of a life dying so that I could eat.

I am not suggesting that other people should do as I did and become a vegan, though. There are certain choices that we all have to make in life, and this was my personal choice. I am well aware that many people have a need to eat meat, for many different reasons.

A Teenager Now

I was about fourteen years old, and just at that age when you really want to be out and about, playing and enjoying yourself, when the next really significant thing in my life happened.

Paul was wanting me to learn about the divine world and all things spiritual, but I had become very rebellious. I was a nightmare, not only to Spirit, but also to my family. When I think back to those times, it is now absolutely plain to me what an ungrateful little scoundrel I was. I was an opinionated and headstrong know-it-all. I thought I knew best, and now I cringe as I remember how crass and selfish I was. There were times when I was downright rude to Paul and to other spirits, and I sometimes wonder why they bothered with me. But they stood by me, right through this most difficult of times. One eventful night, though, something happened that was to change my life forever.

I had moved into the front bedroom, which I was sharing with my brother. By now we had our own beds; this was luxury indeed! My brother's bed stood alongside the back wall, and mine faced the window.

My brother and I were getting along a lot better by now. I was allowed to join in games and get up to the same things as him, like scrumping apples from the allotments. I only ever became a hero once in my teenage years – and that was when I was scrumping apples from the local orchard. I got caught by a copper, but I acted really tough because so many of our schoolmates were there. I was really cheeky to him, and when he clipped me around the ear, I didn't even cry.

At last my brother and I could hold a conversation without resorting to verbal sparring. Even so, he still thought I was weird; later in life he told me that the family thought about putting me in a boarding school so they could all get some respite.

Anyway, my brother and I were talking about a new girlfriend he had – their friendship was to last for years. And yes, even I had a girlfriend by now. So here we were – two men of the world, not long out of short pants, discussing girls. Now that I am many decades more mature and rapidly sailing towards my second youth, those times all seem so laughable, but believe me, they were important then!

We were sitting in our beds chatting away, when suddenly I sat bolt upright in disbelief. I saw a figure floating down from the sky, towards the house. I yelled at my brother to come quickly. He darted out of bed so he could look out the window and see for himself.

"Where is it?" he shouted.

I pointed, but he couldn't see anything.

"You're bleedin' crackers!" he said. "I'm telling Mum you're up to your old tricks again. You're a nutcase!"

To say I was stunned would be an understatement. The figure had stopped in mid-air. As far as I could tell, it was between sixty and eighty feet away from me. I could see it as clear as day. The figure gestured to me to come forward.

The next thing I knew, I was at the side of this figure. Without knowing in a clear-cut way in my mind, and yet somehow still knowing, I understood who he was.

I remember feeling unclean, and very, very ashamed of myself.

I did not look up at him, but rather at the hem of his robe, which appeared blue, and at his feet. He wore a loose type of sandal, which somehow looped over the big toe. I did not see any wounds on his feet.

He spoke to me in a very soft voice, and said: "Why do you deny my Father's gifts to you?"

Then he told me to look at him. What I can tell you, Reader, is this: He was not like any picture I had ever seen of him, nor like any I have ever seen since, even to this day. He was tall and very slim, and had very dark eyes indeed. He had a longish nose, very dark hair, and no beard. He didn't have a particularly handsome face, but he did have a presence that would melt the heart of an angel, and at that moment I fell utterly and totally in love with him. To this day I feel exactly the same, still in that childlike way. I promised there and then that I would serve him all my life, in any way that the Father wished me to.

What a promise! When I think back to that time, I always wonder whether I have done justice to that promise. In all seriousness, and without any false modesty, I doubt that I have achieved my goal.

Then he placed his hand on my head. Suddenly I was back in my bedroom; I climbed into bed feeling ice-cold. I was absolutely exhilarated, yet I also had the feeling that I was not the real me anymore.

Some time later I asked my brother about that night, partly because I was wondering why he hadn't told Mum about it. He said he thought I was bonkers, but he also said that because in some weird way I believed all the strange things I was seeing, I was to be pitied, too. I wasn't sure whether to be happy or angry with him for saying that, but at least it meant I didn't have to confront Mum. Strangely, though, for several weeks after my experience, I had no contact with my spirit friends. I tried everything I knew: I prayed, and I promised all sorts of naive, silly things, but it was to no avail. Spirit only came back to me in their own good time. Paul told me they had been giving me time to reflect upon and to respect the great honour of being a servant.

From then on I did my best to justify the honour I had been given of working with Spirit, but I can assure you that I have fallen down many times, then and now.

Obligation

Like us all, I suppose, I have things in my life that I know I must do, but there are times when I will look for some excuse to justify not doing them. In my case, it can be things like writing letters and returning phone calls. Other times I really don't want to go to meetings, even ones that have been booked for months. Sometimes when I have to fulfil these obligations I just feel like acting like a spoiled child.

One day Paul put me through the greatest embarrassment of my teenage years. I was about to learn a real lesson about obligation and respect.

A tramp asked me for money, and although I had some on me, I refused him, because my money was so hard to come by.

Paul's words to me were harsh: "Take off your coat and give it to him now!"

I was so shocked by Paul's tone of voice that I gave the tramp my coat immediately. I'm sure the old man must have been equally shocked to receive it! Paul made me hand over all my money, too. I then had to go home and tell Mum that I no longer had a coat, or any money. Poor Mum; she must have despaired of me over the years.

Paul told me in a not very kindly way that I had no right to make judgements about people without prior knowledge of their circumstances, and that in doing what he had done, he had let me off very lightly. He may have thought so, but I certainly didn't.

Everything Has Energy

The episode with the coat was far from my only embarrassment. One Sunday afternoon our church organised a treat for all us Sunday School children. We were all townie kids, so to give us a break from our usual surroundings, they took us to a place called the High Mounts, where families would go for picnics and walks. The High Mounts were only a few miles out of town, but when you went there, it felt a bit like you were out in the countryside.

We each had a picnic bag that had been provided by the Sunday School. Most of the picnic bags didn't make it to the High Mounts; they were scoffed long before we got on the coach.

At the High Mounts we kids were allowed to go exploring on our own. My friends and I went off to play the usual game of cowboys and Indians. There were plenty of trees to climb up and hide in, and lots of little caves to explore. As I have said before, I was not a robust child; in fact I was really quite fat. With all that running around, I was out of breath before my slimmer friends, so I went off to the caves to hide and have a rest. I found a small cave and sat down in it. I had only been there for a couple of minutes when I heard some voices coming through the trees, so I ran out of the cave and hid behind a clump of bushes. As a lone boy I didn't want to be found sitting in a cave. Even at the age I was then, I realised it could have looked very strange.

I peeked out from behind the bushes, and I got an awful shock. There were five people there, dressed in such a bizarre way that I felt quite scared. The closest I can describe them is to say they looked like cavemen and cavewomen. I couldn't understand a word they were saying. And even though they were standing only a few feet away from me, they seemed to be totally unaware that I was there. One of the women was holding a big bunch of greenery with a small yellow flower on it, and they all seemed to be quite excited about this.

Then I heard another group of voices. These ones were coming through the trees too, but from a different direction than the first group. This second group sounded completely different, and I could understand what they were saying to each other. A dog was the first from their group to come into my view. It stopped dead in its tracks and started barking at the first group, who were standing in front of the cave. Next to appear were a man and a woman, who had a boy with them. Their dog kept barking. I heard the woman say that a rabbit must have run into the cave. The man told the dog to stop.

Except for the dog, this group was totally unaware of anything unusual going on, and vice versa: The people in front of the cave couldn't see or hear the dog, or the second group of people, who by now were standing only inches away from them.

Suddenly the dog noticed me. There was no way I could hide quietly anymore, and I stepped out from behind the bush. All three – man, woman and child – looked astonished. As for me, I had a face like a beetroot. I muttered something to them about having to go and "spend a penny", and I dashed off as fast as my legs would carry me.

Over the years I have asked many people in my line of work why things like this happen, when they seem to have no relevance at all to the person who witnesses them. I have been given many explanations on the subject, which have generally been as clear as mud.

The only explanation that I have had that has made any sense at all was given to me by a charming spirit friend, who told me that everything has energy, past and present, and that this energy remains, as a kind of chronicle of historical events, which in some cases people are able to tap into. This means that I was seeing some kind of cosmic tape recording of the past that afternoon at the cave. Somehow my present energy linked in with the record of that event. Please remember I am giving a simple explanation for something I don't really understand myself.

Over the years very, very many things have happened to me that appear to be without rhyme or reason, but at least now I have a way of thinking of them that helps me find some sense in them.

Making Ends Meet

By now money was becoming a little easier for the family. Mum was working in a television factory, my sisters were working in a watch factory, and one of my brothers was a trainee painter and decorator.

In those days there were no social security benefits, at least not for the youngest child, so it was important for me to work, to help the family to maintain me. First thing in the morning I did a paper round, then I came back home to wash up after breakfast and make the beds. After school I did an evening paper round, then I rushed home to clean the grate and light the fire. In those days we still cooked on a black-lead range. I would prepare a meal for the workers coming home, and load the washing into the copper boiler. Although we were poor, we always had clean clothes. As the saying used to go, if ever we had to go to hospital, at least we would have clean underwear on.

After all that was done there were always groceries to buy from the shops, then I would dash off to my job at a factory that made potato crisps. I started work at six in the evening, and finished at ten. Then I would run home. I would be back by half past ten to wash up after tea and supper, and do any other jobs that needed doing.

I really started to hate my brother, because by this time he would always be snuggled up in bed. It was too late to go into his room in case I woke him up, so during the week I had to sleep on the sofa in the sitting room – I wasn't even allowed to share his room anymore. It wasn't my poor brother's fault, but I laid the blame for a lot of my troubles at his door. And by the way, I hate potato crisps to this day.

On Saturdays I worked at a rag factory from seven in the morning until four in the afternoon. Of course it was hard work, but there was a pay-off to doing this job: I was able to sell some of the clothes to the people in our neighbourhood. I was sure we had the best-dressed neighbourhood for miles around.

On Sundays I went to early-morning church. I basically went for two reasons only. Firstly, Mum would have been on the warpath if I hadn't gone, and secondly, we had the most wonderful priest you could ever hope for, Father Mason, and I loved seeing him. Other than that I would have rather had the extra time sleeping.

After church, I went to work all day at the fish market. At the end of the day I would break the fish boxes up into bundles of wood. I used an old pushchair to get them all home. Then I would go round from door to door, selling them at two pence for a small bundle and three pence for a large one. It was a real friend to me, that old pushchair. When it finally broke, it got another lease of life as a racing trolley for one of the kids in our street.

By the time I had delivered the wood around the houses I was very, very tired indeed. That was one of the things I really hated about my childhood – the feeling of being permanently tired. If you had asked me at the time what my favourite hobby was, I would have just said sleeping.

All this work brought me in the princely sum of eleven shillings a week. My keep was one pound and five shillings, so I always owed money.

Throughout all this Paul still expected me to keep up my studies. Many, many times I fell asleep while saying my prayers, but when I woke in the morning, Paul would be there to remind me where I had left off. I believe the thing that kept me going was my love for Spirit. What a naive and egotistical little soul I was! Quite the little knight in shining armour!

Another strange thing happened to me one night, after a particularly bad day. I had gone to bed on the sofa and I was saying my prayers, when I burst into tears. I was feeling so sorry for myself, and I really gave it the works. I was thinking how I prayed and did everything Paul asked me to, and I worked so hard, but I never seemed to get anywhere.

All of a sudden I seemed to have jumped out of my body. Well, to be more precise, I was pulled out, because I felt a strong pair of hands holding mine. They were Paul's hands. I found myself in a place that was no place. All I could see was millions of tiny white stars darting around me; everything else was covered in a deep mauve colour. The next thing I knew, I was flying up into the sky, soaring over the houses, and beyond. I seemed to be flying over towns and countries that I never knew existed. I saw people working in fields, but not only that; I also saw famine, war, people weeping, and all sorts of very upsetting things. Then I heard a voice say to me: "Would you exchange your life for the life of any of these people?"

After that experience, I had the feeling I should be glad of my lot, and stop moaning.

Chou-Li

My sixteenth birthday was the happiest occasion I had ever known. You could really say I got the best birthday present I could have wished for. On that day a friend from the spirit world came to join me, and he enriched my life enormously. He still does to this day, and we are the greatest of pals.

I was just about to leave the house to go to work, so I opened the front door. Standing on the step was the smallest person I had ever seen. There he was, a little Chinese man, four foot nothing soaking wet. He had a beautiful smile, and a pigtail that went down past his waist. He was wearing a wonderful Chinese robe, and his first words to me were, "Greetings, I Chou-Li, we very good friends, yes."

From that day on my life changed so much. Chou taught me how to laugh from the heart; in fact he was so funny that I was laughing most of the time. Thank you so much, Chou, good and loyal friend!

In all the years I have known Chou, I have never seen him anything other than happy and smiling. Many people have come to know him over the years, and they all absolutely love him.

Chou taught me that there are no such things as problems, only situations. He said that as soon as you say the word problem your mind accepts a kind of defeat; but the word situation puts the matter in a very different light: your mind feels it can resolve the matter. To this day I live my life by his philosophy; it is a gem of reality that I have taught to many of the people who have come to see me over the years.

Chou taught me always to leave people happy, and with hope, no matter how difficult the situation seems. But the greatest thing he taught me was to always speak the truth, never adding anything or taking anything away. Chou also taught me to make sure that people understand what I am saying to them, so that there is never any confusion in their minds. This was a good lesson for me, because I did not always have the clearest ways of expressing myself when I was young. And that is why I am trying to make my books very simple and unsophisticated –

to tell it like it is, and was. In any case, I wouldn't know how to write in the wonderfully clever ways that other writers do. I try to accept that I'm doing my best.

Chou did a lot of really good and humorous things for me. I was young, and I think I must have been very selfish indeed, but Chou would comfort me and make me laugh. When I felt hard done by, he would bring me back to reality. He would show me what I did have, and how lucky I was to have it. He taught me to look at all the people around me living in the same situation. He also helped me to see that my brothers and sisters and the rest of my family were very normal – that I hadn't come from the "family from hell". As I say, I must have been a very egotistical and selfish young man.

In the first year that I knew Chou, I grew more confident and happy, so much so that I left home and got my own little place. The family expected me to come running back home within a fortnight, but I never went back to live. My little place may only have had one room, but it was mine.

Even so, this turned out to be a very confusing time for me, because now that I was living on my own, I didn't really have anyone else to talk to. I didn't feel comfortable about going back home for visits, and it was impossible to have much of a conversation with anyone there anyway, so basically I only had my spirit friends to talk to. This was my naivety again, but somehow talking to spirit people didn't feel the same as talking to earthly people. Would anyone ever really understand how I was feeling? Later on, I got to know other people in my line of work, and I realised they had gone through a time of having similar thoughts and feelings to mine. But back then, I felt sure I must be the only person who spoke to spirits. Of course my spirit friends all told me that I wasn't, and they told me to go to the churches that are for people like me. So I resolved to go searching.

The Spiritualist Church

One Sunday afternoon when I was feeling low, I was just getting ready to go out for a walk when Chou said to me: "There's a church only a minute away from your place."

"I don't understand what you mean," I said to Chou. "The only building I can see around here is some kind of converted hall."

"Go in, Joseph," said Chou. "Go on, you'll be all right."

So I walked up to the hall. As soon as I got through the doors, a very elderly gentleman greeted me like I was a long-lost grandson.

"We don't get many youngsters in here," he said. "But you are very welcome."

Then he led me to a chair. The chairs were all arranged in a large circle, which I had never seen in a church before, at least not in the ones I had been to.

People kept arriving. It seemed like everyone knew everyone else. I didn't know anyone at all, but everyone was very kind to me.

By the time the service was due to start, every chair was filled. I was starting to feel very apprehensive, though. I tried to see if any of my spirit friends were there, but I couldn't see anyone I knew. I couldn't even see anyone I didn't know.

A very large lady stood up and started speaking. She welcomed everyone, and the service began. I was still very young, of course, but I just thought she was going on and on and on. As I wondered when she would finish, my mind started to drift. In the end I was only taking in the occasional word. I was wishing I hadn't come. I tried to focus on something, so I looked at the centre of the circle. And that was where Chou appeared.

Chou was true to form. He had started dancing round in a really comical way. He was swinging his pigtail around in the air, and being very silly. I tried my hardest not to laugh – I really did try – but out it came. I burst forth in fits of giggles, and the harder I tried to stop, the worse it got. On top of that, I was so embarrassed! I was aware that everyone in the hall was staring at me.

The lady taking the service glared at me. "What do you find so funny, young man? In all my years serving this church, I have never seen such a spectacle! Will you leave now!"

I stood up. But from somewhere in the circle, a little voice spoke. Not far from the big lady who was taking the service sat a little lady. Everyone turned to look at her.

"Sit down, son," she told me. "And you sit down, too," she told the big lady.

We both sat down. Then she said something that made me jump:

"It's not the young man's fault that he laughed out loud. I nearly did myself! There's a little Chinese man standing in the middle of this circle. He's dancing around and clowning about. He was getting weary of listening to our leader's voice, just as I was. Don't you realise this young man is a medium?"

Up until that moment, I had no idea what a medium was. My spirit friends had always said I was a seer, and to this day I think of myself as a seer – someone who sees – but not in the Biblical sense of being a prophet.

Anyway, the service went on, and the little lady,

who was the medium for the evening, asked me to join her. I was very nervous indeed; I wasn't used to facing an audience, and I felt very intimidated by it all. But I did take part in my first public meeting, conveying messages to people.

I did persevere, but I'm afraid I didn't like it very much. Even all these years and hundreds of public meetings later, I still don't enjoy giving out messages in front of an audience. I much prefer seeing people individually and talking with them privately.

The thing I remember most about that evening was a young man from the spirit world who asked me to pass on a message to his mother. He pointed to a lady in the audience and said, "Tell her it's her son. Tell her she's got a rabbit's-foot key ring in her purse that I bought for her the day before my motorbike accident."

You can imagine my dilemma. Here I was at my very first meeting, green as a leaf, but expected to stand up and talk in front of all those people.

"Go on, Joseph," said Chou. "I'm here. Don't be afraid."

So I passed on the message, and to my surprise, the lady opened her purse and pulled out a rabbit's-foot key ring. Everyone applauded, to my surprise.

Everyone – that is – except the big lady, who I'm sure had taken an instant and permanent dislike to me.

It turned out that it was the first time the lady I gave the message to had been in a spiritualist church, so we were both novices together. Even the name was new to me; before that day, I had no idea what a spiritualist church was.

What that day did was to make me feel I wasn't alone. I realised there were other people like me who I could talk to. I'll be forever grateful to that little lady who let me serve with her that evening.

I'm sorry to say, though, that I never learned anything about spirituality from spiritualist churches, despite attending them very many times. I hasten to add that the fault for this is mine and not the churches'. It seems that these churches are very much geared to passing on messages, and this is very important, of course, for it offers proof of the spirit world. And it is only fair to point out that there are many excellent people in these churches who put in a lot of time and effort working for Spirit. In my case, my friends Titus, Paul and Chou teach me nearly everything I need to know about spiritual matters, but as Paul says, we can learn something from everyone to help to steer us on our path to understanding.

The Spiritualist Church

Nevertheless I had lost any real interest in the spiritualist church by the end of the year. I felt I was in the wrong place, so I stopped going.

Go North

One night I fell asleep as usual, but shortly afterwards I was aware of being absolutely wide awake. I seemed to be standing in the middle of the room, and I could see everything around me in its usual place, but someone was sleeping in my bed, so I went over to see who it was. To my horror, I saw a figure lying there that looked like an identical twin to me. In fact it was me. But I was standing up in the middle of the room, so how could I be lying down in my bed at the same time?

Then I realised I had left my body and was astral travelling. Only an instant later, I was standing in front of a huge building with two great big stone lions in front of it. As I looked to my left, I saw a very tall building with a huge bird on top of it. Very clearly I heard a voice say, "Go north, young man. Go north." And the next thing I knew, it was morning.

These words and images kept coming back to me over the weeks, but I couldn't make head or tail of them. My spirit friends were of no help – when I asked them, I was met with silence. But one day a young man came to live in the flat next to mine. His name was Frank, and we became great pals. He was studying at the local college, but Christmas was approaching, and he was going home for the holidays. Knowing I was on my own, he invited me to spend Christmas with his family. They lived in Liverpool. Frank left before me, and I followed on a few days later.

The first thing I saw when I left the railway station was a building with two huge stone lions in front of it. Then I looked to my left and saw a very tall building with a massive stone bird on top of it – the Liver Building.

I had a wonderful Christmas, and to my joy, Frank's mum was very interested in the spirit world. She invited me to a meeting at the house of one of her friends. I was a bit apprehensive about going, but Frank's mum told me it would be fine. We arrived, and while Frank's mum was being greeted by her friends, I looked up and saw a beautiful little girl of about ten or eleven standing on the stairs. I smiled at her, thinking that she must be the daughter of the lady of the house. I also thought she must be going to a fancy dress party; her hair was tied with a huge ribbon on either side of her head, and it fell in ringlets at the front. She was wearing a frilly, calf-length dress, with long pants showing below, and she wore spat shoes.

About a dozen people were sitting in the living room. I quite expected the little girl to follow, in fact I thought she was on her way down the stairs when we arrived. Anyway, the meeting started. To be honest, I don't remember much about it, as it followed the same sort of format as the spiritualist churches. When the meeting was over we had tea, and I asked the lady of the house about her daughter. She looked puzzled, and said she didn't have a daughter. So I asked her about the little girl on the stairs. But then the light dawned! I realised she was a spirit girl. The lady said that this would explain why things kept getting moved or lost. I excused myself to go to the "smallest room", which was upstairs. The little girl was still on the landing, looking lost. I said something to her, but she didn't reply. Paul spoke to me, and asked me to pray for her. This confused me, and

I asked Paul why I needed to pray for her. After all, she was a child, and to me, children are innocent.

Since that talk with Paul, I have learned more about these kinds of appearances.

The little girl was re-enacting an event in her earthly life, and to help her to be able to move on, she needed to tell someone on earth about it. The child was not spending her whole time at the house, but she had been visiting it, in order to build up an awareness of herself on the earthly side of life, ready for her presence to be explained to someone. A little while later Paul confirmed to me that everything had worked out fine for this little girl, and she was now a very happy little soul.

I ended up staying in Liverpool for two years, working as a trainee metallurgist. I was offered the job thanks to a lady who had come to see Frank's mother. This lady said she had had a message from her husband, who was in spirit, telling her to give me a chance.

By now I was living in a large house that had been divided up into several flats. Mine was a small, one-bedroomed flat at the very top. My bedroom looked out onto the house next door, which had stood empty for years, and which Chou had told me I must avoid.

I always wondered why Chou had said this. I was intrigued by the house, and one day while I was looking out my window, I saw lights there and the shadow of a figure. I felt somewhat unnerved, but I couldn't understand why, because since I had got older I had lost any fear of the spirit world. Being stubborn, or maybe dense, I went downstairs. I felt a sense of horror, but I willed myself to go next door.

I walked through the back yard. No doubt at some stage children had played there. The back door to the house was open. I crept inside.

The smell of damp and rotting wood was everywhere, but strangely enough, once I was inside the house, I didn't feel so bad. I went through a doorway into a hall, and then into a front room. There was only a dim light coming from the windows, as they were boarded up. I turned to leave the room, but I felt – rather than saw – a presence standing in the doorway. It was definitely a presence I felt none too happy about.

I spoke to it, saying, "Who are you, and what do you want? Let me pass." I was trying to be all brave and not show any fear. Why I said "let me pass", I really don't know. This presence hadn't tried to stop me from doing anything, but I must have felt it would challenge me. Deep down I was feeling very afraid.

As I stared into the space ahead of me I could just about make out the shape of a person, but I couldn't tell whether it was male or female.

By now I was almost overwhelmed by a feeling of dread. I was desperate to get out of the house, but just then I heard a voice telling me to go into the cellar. There was no way I was going to do that, not even for a gold bar, but I felt this "thing" almost pulling me towards the cellar by some kind of force. I began to feel that I was in a trance-like state. I tried with all my might, and managed to call out "Jesus, help me!" Then I saw Titus standing at my side, and I knew I was all right. But I can tell you, I left the house a lot faster than I had gone in.

I got a right dressing-down from Titus and Chou, who said that since they knew far more about the spirit world than I did, I had better listen in future.

Some time later the house was knocked down to make way for a new place. When the foundations were being dug in the cellar area, a body was found. I understand it had been there for years.

My Other Grandmother

I was now at a stage when I was asking myself what I should be doing with my life. I was receiving so much help from my spirit friends that I felt I was living more in their world than in mine. I felt I wanted to have some life of my own, and do things for myself. I was at that stage when young men need to be going out with young ladies, going dancing perhaps, having fun and making merry. My brothers and sisters were enjoying life – they knew where they were going. They were full of fun, and even Mum had a man friend by now. Here I was, a young man, spending all my time learning and dealing with spiritual matters.

One day I was sitting on a park bench opposite some tennis courts. The clouds darkened, and I expected it to rain. But instead, a ray of light came out of the clouds, and it flooded the whole tennis court. Then I noticed a figure walking towards me. It was just a tennis player, I thought, and the light was just a normal ray of sunlight, breaking through the clouds. But then the figure stopped in front of me, and I realised it was a lady dressed in old-fashioned clothes. She was very elderly, but she had the most regal stance about her. In fact, apart from the clothes that she wore, she reminded me very much of the old Queen Mary.

"Hello, I am your grandmother," she said. "And I am here to help you. You have been chosen to work for us, and for the people who are in need of us. You will teach, until the time is right for us to reveal your role as a servant of the cause that one day will be so dear to your people."

At that time of my life, I hardly felt these words were much help to me; in fact they upset me. My needs were of a personal nature, so what she was saying seemed quite irrelevant, and not very important, either. If I wanted help at all, it would have been help with doing something in my life that I enjoyed doing for me. This sounds so selfish, and it was.

Grandmother went on to say, "We are going to train you for trance – deep trance."

Once again I had no idea what she was talking about, but she continued:

"The time is coming when the people you meet in your life will need more than just messages relayed to them. We need to make personal contact with people in your world, in order to pass on our knowledge. We need to allow our wise ones to help your people."

I loved seeing the lady who said she was my grandmother; she had a very beautiful presence about her. But to my mind, it felt like the wrong time for me to hear the things she was telling me. She didn't seem to understand my needs, and I didn't really want to hear what she had to say. In fact, hearing her words turned me cold, and made me a little resentful that I wasn't being allowed some kind of personal life, unlike everyone else I seemed to know.

Later that day I phoned Mum and asked her about my grandmother. I told her about the lady who had spoken to me, and Mum said I was describing my father's mother, who died a few months after Mum and Dad met. So this lady was indeed my grandmother.

Life went on, much the same as usual. My spirit friends made no mention of the trance thing that my grandmother had spoken about – well, not for several years, anyway. In my life I have learned that my perception of time and Spirit's perception of time are as different as chalk and cheese. Once I asked quite a simple question about my personal life, and I was told someone would come to answer it for me. Someone did indeed come and answer my question, a full twenty-three years after I had asked it.

The Churchyard

One day I was on my way home from the city centre. As I was walking down the street towards the bus stop, I went past a church that stood on the other side of the road. For some silly reason, I felt drawn to cross the road and look at an old tomb in the churchyard. It seemed a ridiculous idea, really. I had passed this churchyard dozens of times before, and I had never felt the slightest inclination to go in.

It was autumn, so the leaves were falling. They crackled underfoot as I dashed across the yard. I got to the tomb, but I found it was broken and dilapidated, so with a morbid sense of curiosity that only the young seem to have, I peeked inside, to see if I could see a coffin, or a body. I nearly jumped out of my skin when I heard a voice behind me say, "You won't find me in there, only my body."

The Churchyard

I turned around quickly and saw a tall, youngish man standing about two feet away from me. He had a pleasant face, and he was wearing a long overcoat. But before I could reply to him, he had turned and walked away. Worst of all, I got the distinct feeling that he was an unsavoury kind of soul.

By the time I had recovered my composure, he was out of the gate. He looked back at me, and it was only at that moment that I realised what he had actually said. I also realised I hadn't heard him walk up to me or away from me. If he had been human, I would have heard the sound of his footsteps on the autumn leaves that lay thick on the ground.

I asked Chou what it was all about, and he told me that I looked at the spirit world through rose-coloured glasses.

Chou was right, of course, but then again, why would I ever think of people from the spirit world as anything other than lovable? Apart from that one time I went into the abandoned house in Liverpool when I shouldn't have, I had only ever met lovable spirits, and they had shown me nothing but goodness and kindness. But I needed to learn that there are elements that are not so good in the spirit world, too, just as there are on Earth. Not everything is perfect where people are concerned. I had thought that the young man seemed quite pleasant, but it is true that all that glitters is not gold. After all, when we take our promotion to the spirit world, we do not automatically become angels. We still take our personalities with us, for better or worse. In my book *Talking with Spirit* I explain what happens to people who have led a life of shadows.

Developing a Personal Relationship with God

By now a lot more was happening in my personal life, and I won't bore you with the details of all that, but I have to say that I still felt in conflict with myself. I was still not happy with the feeling that I was the odd one out from the rest of the community. I would watch people doing normal, everyday things like going out in the evenings and socialising, but I myself was still doing very little of that, and to be quite honest, I felt like I was some kind of alien. Religion and the church still meant a great deal to me: they were very much a part of my personal psyche – of who I was – and I felt that my contact with the spirit world meant I was being disloyal to them.

I could not forget my early childhood and the priest at our church, for he was the one man I knew who truly served God and the people in his parish.

He did deal with spiritual matters, but he also did all the practical things he could to help improve people's daily lives, and his example showed me how I should live my life. When I looked at what I was doing in my life, I certainly didn't seem to be doing very much in a hands-on kind of way. Wonderful spiritual things were happening to me, but I felt like I was playing at life. In fact where spirituality was concerned, I felt like I was the one who always got the icing on the cake while other people were doing all the baking.

I had a deep need to feel accepted by the church, although as time went by I realised that it was not actually religion that I was trying to come to terms with. One part of me needed to feel accepted by the people I respected. Another part of me needed to understand that I was a person in my own right, and that my life had a purpose. Once again Chou came to my rescue, and his truth has sustained me all of my life. Chou said that there are countless religions in the world, all of which in their own way can lead to God, but what is important to God is one's personal faith in him and one's relationship with him.

Chou said God respects all creeds and all denominations, and there is truth in the Bible, but you can only fulfil your life if you live it through inner faith, and through your personal relationship with God.

Religions exist for the group mind – for those who think and feel alike – but even religious or church-going people must live their lives according to their personal faith in God.

God speaks to us individually, and sends his love to us in a personalised way. He does not treat us collectively. He treats us as individual souls, because that is how he knows us.

There is no compromise with God. It matters not if we are people of light or of darkness; God's love is there for each and every soul. It is our faith that keeps us on our path.

Religions have destroyed kingdoms, but faith has saved souls.

Once more Chou had given me knowledge that would let me make sense of the world around me. I felt much freer now to pursue as many aspects of a spiritual life as I was capable of.

Please don't get the idea that I was a goody-goody, because as a young man, I had my moments, I can assure you. In fact, there were lots of moments – far too many for my own good! But I certainly became more comfortable with myself once I realised that it was God that I had to please.

Nobody There

By this stage in my life I was taking regular public meetings. I was very conscious of what Spirit expected of me, but I still got a shock one particular Sunday.

The meeting was about to begin. I looked out onto a sea of expectant faces; everyone was waiting for me to get started. I addressed the gathering, then I waited, as I always did, for Paul to tell me everything was ready. But Paul wasn't there. I could neither see him nor hear him. I just stood there like a lemon, and before long, I was wishing that the floor would open and swallow me up. I kept looking around, hoping that someone – anyone at all, in fact – would come and speak to me. But I could only see blankness. I had to stand there in front of all these people and apologise to them because I couldn't make contact.

I must admit that for a few fleeting seconds it occurred to me to make up something to say, and tell the audience I was getting messages when I wasn't. But I realised that as ever, I was to tell the truth – never adding anything or taking anything away, and never making anything up. At that moment Paul spoke to me. I don't think I have ever been so relieved in my working life.

"Joseph, just don't take us for granted," he said.

Then I had to tell everyone in the audience that I had just been put in my place, but the meeting could start now. I can assure you that from that day on, I was always very mindful of not taking the spirit world for granted.

My Brother's Car

I would also like to tell you about something that happened when I was a little older. It was a strange experience, but a wonderful one too, although it was very frightening at the time.

I had been to see my brother, and he was giving me a lift back to my place. We chatted as we drove along. I felt slightly uneasy, so I tried to work out why, but I couldn't. I sent out thoughts to my guides to see if I could pick anything up, or if they might tell me why I felt that way. They gave me no answer.

My brother turned left into a road that led down a very steep hill. I was talking away, but when I turned to him, I saw that he had gone absolutely silent. The car had picked up an awful lot of speed.

"What are you going so fast down this hill for?" I asked. "Don't you think that's really dangerous?"

My Brother's Car

"The brakes have gone! The steering's gone!" he shouted.

We just kept going faster and faster. There was a grass verge on the far side of the road, but when my brother tried to steer the car towards it, nothing happened, so he opened his door, yelling "Jump!" – which he did. To my horror, I saw him rolling along the roadway.

The car was hurtling down the hill by now. I could see the main road looming up ahead. Somehow I would have to stop the car before it reached the stream of traffic, but I couldn't. I thought my time had come, and I closed my eyes. This was it. As I had been taught, I said, "Into the Lord's arms I commend my soul." I felt a slight panic as I thought of my family, and how they would feel.

As I reached the main road the wheels started to scream. The car was still going very fast as it swung round the corner, but then it promptly pulled up and stopped. I was in some state of shock, I can assure you. I don't know how long I stayed there for, but the next thing I knew my brother was racing round the corner to the car. He pulled the door open with a look of astonishment on his face, saying, "I thought you were dead! I thought you were dead! How the hell did you steer the car round a corner like that? How did you manage to stop it? The brakes and the steering had gone!" He tested the steering wheel. It just spun around endlessly.

"I didn't!" I said. "It just happened that way!"

"Don't give me that rubbish about your spooks, because I don't believe in them!" he said.

He sat back down in the car, though – more out of shock than anything else, I think – and the strangest thing happened: the engine started up on its own. Neither of us knew what emotion to feel. My brother jammed his foot on the brake out of pure reflex action. The brake worked fine. He tested the steering again, and it was fine.

My brother has often told that story back to me over the years, and when he has had a few in the pub he tells it to his friends, so I know that somewhere inside him he believes that there is something beyond this world.

The New House

On my first day in the house where I was to live for many, many years, I saw an elderly lady on the landing, just as I was about to go up the stairs. I had my hands full, and my mind was busy trying to sort out where to put everything, when she called out to me, "What are you doing in my house?"

"No dear, this is my house now," I replied.

As I went up the stairs, she started heading towards the back bedroom, so I followed her.

"This is my house, and this is my bedroom," she told me adamantly.

It took a while, but eventually I got her to understand that my family and I would be living there now, but she was welcome to stay as long as she liked. She told me her name was Sarah.

Some time later two friends came to stay, neither

of whom believed in the spirit world. The back bedroom was spare, so at the end of the evening they went there to sleep. Pretty soon after, I heard them shouting for me to come upstairs. There was a real urgency in their voices. When I got there I found them sitting on the bed, clinging to each other. They were staring towards one corner of the room, and they looked terrified. Sarah was sitting there in the armchair smiling away, quite well aware of the reaction she was causing.

"Oh, it's only Sarah," I said. "She lives here."

From that day on, my friends were firm believers in a world after this one. In fact they became a great help to me in my work, over many years. I'll just backtrack a bit to my first day in the house, though.

After a whole day of loading and unloading, and finding places for the furniture and appliances and everything else, I was exhausted. The family had gone to bed, and I was relaxing in an armchair in front of the big window, watching TV. Suddenly, to my surprise, a group of monks passed by, right in front of me. They circled around the room, then went out through the kitchen door. They didn't even seem to realise I was there. I jumped up and made for the kitchen, to see where they had gone.

One monk stood in the kitchen, tall and slim. But I couldn't see his face because it was covered by his hood, and this made me feel uneasy. When he spoke it was in a cultured voice, but he had a very peculiar way of speaking English.

"Dig deep in the garden, and you will find a key. When you have found it, I will tell you what it is for," he said. Then he walked straight through the back door, which was locked shut.

So much was going on in my life at the time that I put this encounter to the back of my mind. But one night when I went outside to bring some washing in, I was startled to see the same monk again. He was standing at the bottom of the garden now, by the back gate. I refused to listen to him this time until I could see his face, and he obliged by dropping his hood.

I saw that he was a man of middle years, with quite a thin face. To be honest, he wasn't someone I'd like to meet in a dark alley. Nevertheless, he had complied with my wishes by letting me see his face. This time he said: "Dig here. Dig very deep. Trust me." And then he just disappeared.

The back of the house was close to a city wall of great historic interest, and just over the wall was part of an ancient monastery. I had plenty of doubts about digging so close to the wall, and once again I chose to ignore the matter, but the monk would not go away.

A few weeks later my nephew came to stay with my family and me. While he was with us, he had a dream one night that a monk came up to him and told him to dig in the garden, in a particular place. I asked my nephew to show me where, and he pointed to the exact same spot that the monk had been telling me about. So I let him dig.

He dug for days and days, and the hole kept getting deeper and wider, until in the end I had to put some shoring in. I was starting to get really worried by this stage, and ordered that no more digging be done.

"Trust me!" said the monk, when he appeared to me again. As far as I was concerned, that had worn a bit thin by now. But in the end I had to eat my words, for my nephew did find the key. It was one of those big, old keys that were used to open church doors. And I was genuinely excited about the find, but I had practical matters on my mind, too, such as filling in the chasm in the back garden – a chasm which the neighbours all thought was wonderful, because they got to dump all their rubbish in it. To this day, if you dig in the garden, you will find old tyres, bedsteads, mattresses, and all sorts of odds and ends. It took months to get the garden looking something like a garden again.

The monk did return, and he did tell me what the key was to, but to date I have not gone to find the cask he spoke of because it is buried on private land. I have left instructions in my will about where to find it.

She is Safe and Sound

I was in the kitchen one day washing up, when I looked up and saw a very large lady standing in the doorway. "My son is coming to see you," she said, "and he will give you a red rose."

I thanked her and told her I would keep it in mind. Over the years I have got used to being given messages for people I haven't met; I always meet them sooner or later.

Well, one of my friends called to see me one day, and he brought a young man of about nineteen or twenty with him. When the young man was introduced to me, I realised that he was the one the large lady in the kitchen doorway had been talking about.

I was able to tell him exactly what had been worrying him about his mother's death, and even describe her to him. From then on, he knew she was safe and sound. What a change came over him! It was as if a ton had been lifted from his shoulders.

When he left, I got on with some boring accounts. But there was a knock at the door, and there stood the young man again. He presented me with a red rose, and had a very embarrassed look on his face. I thanked him, and invited him back in for a cup of tea. That's my answer to most things: "Have a cup of tea!" And from that day on, he became like a son to me.

I believe any seer will tell you that you make very dear friends in this kind of work – friends who are there when you need them, or who are just there, with their warmth and love.

Animals

I'm just a complete nutcase where animals are concerned. What a joy they have been to me!

At this time of my life we had three cats in the house. We had had them all since they were kittens. They were all black cats and had all been strays, and they lived with us for years and years.

One of the cats was a real character. He had a crooked ear, so we called him Mr Wonky Ear. He was the sort of friend you would want to prop up a bar with on a Saturday night, and would pick a fight just for the fun of it, but I loved him with all my heart. He always knew when Spirit were around, because he would stare, follow something around the room, spit and curse, and then fly out through the cat flap. There was no way would he have anything to do with Spirit.

The second cat was wonderful too, and very different from Mr Wonky Ear. When he was a very little kitten I used to get up every two hours to feed him with an eyedropper. I would carry him around in my jumper to keep him warm, too. He was spoiled rotten – definitely a champagne cat – but he was such a lovable soul. Whenever anyone came to see me, from either side of life, he would be there, all purrs, asking for his tummy to be tickled. He so loved Spirit, and often he would see Spirit before I did. If there was no one else in the room and I saw him purring away and going into his tickle-me mode, I knew there was a good chance I would see someone soon. And it was quite something to see the looks on friends' and neighbours' faces when the cat was rolling all over the sofa enjoying being tickled, with no visible hand tickling him.

I loved the youngest cat to bits too. She just didn't care about anything, as long as she was fed and cuddled and she ruled the house – which she always did.

We also had a budgie that was hardly ever in his cage – he only slept and fed there. And not once did he offer to fly away when the doors and windows were open. Instead, he sat on the window ledges and watched the world go by. The cats didn't bother him, because the few times they had tried, he had made them sorry with a quick peck on the nose.

The rest of my family were crazy about dogs; as I am too, of course.

The White Season

I always think back to this day with a sense of wonder. I was secretary to a church at the time, although I really only belonged to the church because a group of my friends needed someone to look after the administrative side of things, and as I had some experience of keeping accounts they thought I would be a good choice. Also, the church was wanting to attract more young people into its ranks. I had been involved in schools for years, so they thought I might be of some use. To be honest, I think I was last-chance Joe, the one they asked after everyone else had said no. Anyway, one particular evening after church, I was chatting with a group of young people in their twenties, and they asked me if I could give them proof that the spirit world exists.

"Seek, and ye shall find," I told them. Indeed in

my heart I so wanted them to see proof – not for my sake, because I had seen mine, but for their sakes. How this might come about, though, I had no idea.

Then Titus said to me, "In the white season they will have their proof."

It was June at the time, so this message seemed pretty unhelpful in the short term. I passed it on, of course, and they accepted they would have to wait until winter, but in the meantime, they at least wanted to know what form the proof would take. But Titus wouldn't say, so there wasn't really anything I could tell them.

We drank our tea, and I knew they felt let down. And to be honest, if I had been in their shoes, I know I would have felt the same. We left the church and started to walk home in a group.

Just then, it started to snow. We were all amazed that it should snow when summer was just around the corner. Then the whole group, plus all the passers-by, heard my name being called across the sky three times. Everyone, including total strangers, looked skywards to see where the voice was coming from.

The snow stopped falling as quickly as it had started. One of the group said, "Now we've had our proof of the spirit world. It has snowed in the middle of June, so for us it's the white season. And we have heard a voice call across the sky; there is no way that something like that could have been faked."

I prayed a silent thank you to God.

I am well aware that snow occasionally falls in June, but you wouldn't normally hear a voice calling across the sky in any month. Even today I struggle to believe it really happened. I could accept it more easily if it had happened to someone else.

As far as the group was concerned, a few of them went on to work hard for Spirit over the years, developing their natural gifts and becoming wonderful seers.

Spirit Children

Meeting with spirit children has given me some wonderfully happy times over the years. They say that in show business you should never work with children (or with animals, for that matter). But in my kind of work you have to, and you want to, too, for all the joy and fun they bring.

Maureen is a very bubbly little girl who comes to see me regularly, and the strange thing is that she loves everything to be coloured red. No matter what it is, it just has to be in red.

When she arrives she always has a mischievous smile on her face, and she says to me, "I know a secret!" So I play a little game with her. Maureen passes on a snippet of information to me that is to the advantage of someone I know, and through thoughts and love, I send her something she likes – maybe a little doll, or a hoop, or a puzzle… In red, of course.

There is also a young lad of sixteen who is fascinated by the fact that he can get in touch with Earth, and talk to a real person, as he calls me. Of course I always tell him that he is a real person too.

When I was young, I had a very poignant visit late one night from a little spirit child. I had gone to bed and I was in the middle of saying my prayers, when I felt some pressure at the foot of the bed. I took no notice because I assumed it was one of the cats, but as I went on with my prayers I became aware of a leg pressing against mine. It felt solid to me, but I couldn't see anything. I reached further down the bed, and there was a little baby's bottom. I heard a giggle.

"Hello," I said. "You've come to see Joseph. Are you nice and warm?"

I heard another giggle. It sounded like a very young child, so I patted its leg, and said that after my prayers I would tell it a story. But then I felt the pressure release from my leg, as if the child had moved away.

"Goodbye," I said. "Come and see me again."

Two days later I learned that my sister's little boy had passed away – on the same night that my little visitor had come.

It was very sad that I couldn't tell my sister about the visit, but I knew she wouldn't have believed me. She needed me to be there for her with my feet on the ground, showing my love and support in a very practical kind of way. I did tell her years later, but even then she thought I was just saying it to help her get over her loss.

By that time in my life I had a lovely home and a family of my own, who are so dear and kind to me. Many of my family are not my birth family, but they are every bit as precious to me. I thank God for them every day.

In the extended family we have been lucky enough to be able to help other people, some of whom have been without a family or a home, but have nevertheless gone on to a successful life.

What Am I Doing Here?

One Sunday night I was sitting watching television, when my guide Chou-Li told me I should get up, and go to one of the local churches.

"Chou," I said. "You know I'm not keen on those kinds of churches."

But Chou said, "Just do it, Joseph. Why do you have to question everything?"

I had just made myself comfortable, so reluctantly and not very graciously I got up and went out. I arrived at the church and sat down in the circle, still wondering what on earth I was doing there.

I could see the leader looking at me, and the next thing I knew, he was asking me if I would like to take the service. "Oh, that's very kind of you," I said, "but I'm happy to chip in from here." I made a mental note to repay Chou later.

The service started. I was still wondering why I was there when the door opened and an Indian man came in. He was quite little, and he looked very unsure of himself. I beckoned him over to me and pulled a chair into the circle for him. He sat down, but all through the service I could sense his unease. The service ended, and as usual, people gathered around me, but I thought that couldn't be what I had gone there for. Then I glanced over to where the Indian man was sitting. He was on his own. No one had spoken to him, or even offered him a cup of tea, so I excused myself and went over to him.

"Hello, I'm Joseph," I said, and sat down next to him.

He told me his name, and explained that this was his first time ever in a church, as he'd only been to places of worship of his own religion before. I asked him why he had chosen to come to our church, and he replied, "I actually don't know what I'm doing here. I was sitting at home, and I felt a great urge to go out for a walk. I was passing this church, and the next thing I knew, I found myself inside. Then I was too embarrassed to leave because you'd called me over to you. It's strange, though, because for years I've needed to know what happens after you die… if there's another world after this one..." Well, I invited him home for coffee, and after chatting until about three in the morning, he went home. He went on to become a faithful friend and a loyal worker for the spirit world.

One time he went on a holiday back to India, and while he was there he visited a guru. The two talked about my friend's life in Britain. Then the guru told my friend about me, describing me exactly, even down to my name, and saying that I was a guru too. I don't know about that, but the other things he told my friend were accurate.

One Friday evening my friend's father came to see me. He was the most materialistic of people, and I am not into telling fortunes, but I have been taught never to turn anyone away, so I tried my best for him. Well I was shocked, for his mother appeared, and told me to say that in a few hours he would be very rich and have two new cars. This sounded very odd to me. To be honest, I didn't believe it; I thought she must have her timeframes muddled up. I felt very unhappy about the whole thing, but I still had to pass on what had been said.

The next day I had a phone call from my friend's father. He was beside himself with excitement. He told me he had just heard he'd won a Spot the Ball competition and two new cars. You can call me a doubting Thomas, but I have to say, I was stunned!

Back to School

I now jump ahead many years. By this time I was a senior social worker at a school for disturbed children. The school was in the countryside and surrounded by farms. At one time the land and the buildings had been owned by a lord, but he had gifted them to the city for the benefit of the people.

One of my last duties at night was to do a final walk around the school to check on all the children. Once that was done, I would often go for a walk in the grounds to relax. There were stables within the school grounds, although these days the gardeners were using them as garden sheds. One particular night I went and sat down by the stables. I had been there for a while and I was lost in thought, as I often am, when I heard what I thought was the sound of a cart coming up the back lane into the school grounds.

Farmers sometimes worked very late, and as I say, I had my mind on other things, so I didn't take much notice at first. When I looked down the lane, I saw that the cart was all lit up with bright lights. But I still didn't think there was anything particularly unusual about it until it was about twenty yards away. It was then that I realised it was actually a horse-drawn coach with lanterns on each side. I was astonished! As the coach flew past me I saw its driver in what I thought was seventeenth-century attire. The coach reminded me of those old cowboy stagecoaches, but it was bigger. It was being pulled by four dark-coloured horses. Inside it sat a lady, who looked as startled to see me as I was to see her. All this was over in seconds. I raced back to the main buildings.

In my mind I tried to make connections between the stagecoach and the school's past. Certainly there was a very old mansion house in the grounds, where the school staff lived, including myself, but it didn't quite belong to the same era as the sight I had just seen.

This experience remains a mystery to me as I never got a definitive explanation about it, but I can only assume I had seen another 'historical playback', the same way I'd seen the cave dwellers when I was a child.

Two days later in the staff quarters I met an elderly lady on the stairs while I was walking to my flat. She just smiled at me and passed on her way. When I mentioned her in the staff room the next day, I was told I must have seen the 'Grey Lady'. It seems to me that a lot of places have a grey or a white lady, but I'm not so sure about this one… she was dressed in black.

During my years at the school I saw many strange things, but one of the nicest things I saw, year after year, was the blooming of the daffodils. Every spring the ground would become a sea of daffodils; they were the most glorious sight. There were so many daffodils that the school used to sell some to help raise funds. And there was one particular copse that I often used to walk through where they grew even more profusely than everywhere else.

One clear spring morning I was walking through this copse, listening to the birds singing, when suddenly I heard a voice say, "Hello, are you enjoying the daffodils?"

I turned around to see a lady standing quite close to me. I was in the middle of the countryside and I didn't expect anyone would be around, so I was a bit startled.

"Yes," I said. "Yes, I am. Very much, thank you." Then I said, "I hope I'm not trespassing."

"Oh no, it's fine," she replied. "My husband and I planted these daffodils many, many years ago. Now it's my daughter who plants them."

"Oh," I said. "So your daughter's the one who kindly lets us sell the daffodils for the school funds, then. That's very good of her. Do you live in the big house?"

The big house was a farmhouse that stood in the fields a little further on.

"I did," she said, "but I don't live there now."

She walked a little way with me. Everything seemed very peaceful, and I didn't sense anything unusual at all, but suddenly she said to me, "You have work to do! What are you doing at this school? Isn't it about time you stopped shilly-shallying around and got on with what you're supposed to be doing?"

I shook my head, hardly believing what I had just heard. I turned to her to say "What do you mean?" But she had vanished into thin air.

Another strange thing that happened while I was at the school involved a huge black dog that appeared three times. I remember the first time especially well.

There was a beautiful canal with a little bridge over it about half a mile away from the school. I used to like to go there occasionally so I could paint the scenery, or should I say try to! On this particular day it was sunny and warm, and I was looking over towards some farmland and trees; it was a calm and beautiful landscape. I had my back to the lane and I was trying to work out which scene to paint, when suddenly I heard the footsteps of an animal behind me. I thought a cow or a sheep must have got out from one of the fields. But when I turned around and looked, I realised it was actually a huge black dog, standing about six feet away from me and staring at me.

My heart was in my mouth. There was nowhere to run to – in case I had to – and it looked so fierce. We just stared at each other. I gave a glance around to see if the owner might be there – I was hoping someone would call the dog back – but there was no one. It was just the dog and me. After a few moments I picked up a crumb of courage and spoke to it.

"Hello, boy! Good dog, good dog," I said, in as calm a voice as possible. Where were my spirit friends when I needed them? The dog was completely still, just standing and staring at me. This went on for about two minutes. But then it barked, so I shot off in the opposite direction, up the lane. I looked back after a few seconds to see if it was chasing me, but to my astonishment, it was nowhere to be seen. There was open countryside all around, so I would have seen it easily if it had run over the fields. I looked this way and that as I walked back to the bridge, wondering if it had gone down the embankment or along the canal, but it had just disappeared. I was concerned, and quite nervous, really, because the whole time I was walking back to the school I kept thinking the dog might reappear. Perhaps it was lying in wait for me, about to pounce.

When I passed the same way the next day on my way to the village, I found that the wall of the bridge had been knocked down into the canal. I enquired in the village, and I was told that a drunk driver had lost control of his car and hit the wall. I had been at that spot earlier on in the day, not during the pub's opening hours, but if the dog had let me paint in peace, I would have stayed there many hours. I wondered if the dog had been there to warn me of the impending danger.

The second time I saw the dog I was walking along the canal's towpath. It was about fifty feet ahead of me, and just standing there in the middle of the path. I slowly walked towards it, but it stood its ground, and it had the same fierce look on its face as before.

"Good boy... Where are you from?" I asked. It looked like it was understanding what I was saying. Then it lay down, with its head on its paws. It was still staring at me. I came nearer and nearer until I was about ten or fifteen feet away. The dog barked, but this time it sounded like it was pleased to see me. I still felt very nervous, but I came a little nearer to see if it had a collar on, half wondering if it might have been abandoned. I was sure in my heart that the dog was not of this world, but my spirit friends have always taught me to check everything as much as is possible, so I couldn't leave any potentially important details to chance. I kept approaching, but the dog was not prepared for me to come any closer; it jumped up and dashed into a hedge. I went to see where it had gone to, but it had completely disappeared. I looked for a gap in the hedge that it could have dashed through, but there was no gap.

The third time the dog appeared, I didn't see it myself. I was walking along the lane one evening, heading back from the village to the school, when the local vicar drove past in the opposite direction.

He tooted his horn and I waved. As he passed he wound down his window and asked me where on earth I had got such a huge dog. I just smiled and said it wasn't actually mine. The dog was making sure I got back to school safely – unbeknownst to me until that moment.

A couple of years later I was talking about the dog with my mother, who as an elderly lady was becoming a believer in the spirit world. She told me that when she was about nine years old a huge black dog had stopped her from playing near a well in the garden. The dog gave her such a fright that she ran in to tell her mother. Her mother told her that the dog was a family protector, that one person in each generation saw it, and not to be afraid.

I asked Mum why she had never mentioned this before. She said it was because she had seen lots of things in her early childhood that were strange and unexplained, which she had assumed must be evil. "That was why I got so angry when you started to see things too," she explained. Parents can be so irrational sometimes!

After the three appearances that I have described, I did not see the dog again. I have asked Chou to tell me more about it, but all he will say is that the animal is a wonderful friend to the family. So I have no idea if it was owned by one of my ancestors, or if it just turns up at occasional moments, as it did to me. Certainly I like to think that it belongs in our family, but I'm not sure whether it actually does or not – it might just be wishful thinking on my part.

While I was at the school, one of my duties was to take a group of children to the local church every other week. One Sunday a wonderful thing happened. There was a child in my group who was particularly hyperactive, and quite disruptive, so I said to him, "You must be very good today, because we're going to church to see God."

We all set off for the village, and the little boy behaved impeccably. We went into the church and sat down, and still he was on his best behaviour. The service began. The boy kept quiet for about the first five minutes, but then he started to get hyperactive.

"Ssh! Be quiet!" I kept whispering to him.

"I can't see God!" he replied. "Where's God? I don't know where he is!"

The service went on. After a little while, I noticed that the boy had gone silent. I looked at him, and saw him staring at the stained-glass window that depicted Christ on the cross. To be honest, I was just glad that he was quiet.

The service came to an end, and I gathered all the children together outside. The little boy was still quiet as we walked back to school, and as I held his hand, I said to him, "You were very good in church today. I'm very pleased."

"You're right," he said to me. "I did see God."

"Oh, that beautiful picture on the stained-glass window," I said. "Yes, that's Jesus."

"No, I saw God," he said.

"What do you mean, you saw God?" I asked.

"You told me I would see God, and I've seen God," he said.

So I said to him, "Explain to me what you mean. What did he look like?"

"He had a beautiful face," said the child, "and he was all shining with light. He told me that I was a good boy. And he said that when I'm a big boy, the time will come when I will come to your house and you will help me."

"Did he say anything else?" I asked.

"No," said the boy. "After that I just watched him, because he was listening to what the man at the front was saying." He obviously meant the minister who was reading the service.

I still don't know to this day what the boy saw. He believed he was going to see God in the church, so I like to believe his prayer had been answered in some way and he had seen an angel.

Something strange happened another night while I was on duty at the school, but this time it was something that completely unnerved me. I was walking round doing my final check, and it was about eleven o'clock. I went into a dormitory where three boys should have been sleeping, but I found that one of the beds was empty. I looked in all the usual places – the toilets, the day rooms, and the other dormitories, but to no avail. As I searched, I locked up all the doors behind me. This was a school rule, which had been instituted as a safety measure because we were in the countryside. I kept searching, now passing through the dining room.

The windows of the dining room ran from the floor to the ceiling. I looked out through them, across the courtyard to the big house, and got a shock. The roof of the big house had a parapet, and in the moonlight I could see a figure walking across it. I imagined that the figure might be the missing boy, sleepwalking. I started to panic. I dashed down the stairs to the big house. I ran up the outside fire escape, which led to the roof. I was afraid of what might happen if I didn't get the figure down off the roof, and at the same time I was afraid of wakening it, in case that caused it to fall.

I watched the figure walk towards me. It was indeed the boy who was missing from his bed. I waited until he was within grabbing distance. I noticed that his eyes were wide open, but they seemed glazed over, and he was staring straight ahead. I took hold of his legs, then I spoke very gently to him, asking him if he was all right. No answer came from him, so I asked him what he was doing.

A voice that was definitely not his said, "I am looking for the enemy."

I was astonished. I asked him which enemy he meant, but he said no more.

It took quite a long time to bring the boy down from the roof. I led him back into the school and to his bed, and I said to whoever the soul was: "You must leave him now, and never return to him again. What you did was very dangerous." At that, the boy closed his eyes, as in sleep.

The next day I asked him if he had slept well, and he said he had.

"You didn't have any nightmares, then?" I asked.

But he said that he didn't, so I asked him no more questions.

I tried to find out if there had been some building or other on the site where the big house now stands, but I ended up drawing a blank. I already knew that about a mile and a half from the school there is a hill that a Saxon fort once stood on, and I wondered whether this soul was keeping watch over the fort, and looking out for enemies. Then again, the whole area is very ancient, with a Roman road nearby, so this raises more theories. I was intrigued by the matter, but every time I asked Chou about it, he would simply say nothing.

I had one of the most awful experiences in my life one night while I was walking back from the village. I had been to the shop for some cigarettes, and for some odd reason I decided to walk up some little-used lanes to get back to the school. This route took me past the church. Being a typical country church, it had a graveyard beside it; I had to pass that too. The graveyard was old and somewhat neglected, but in the daytime it had a rustic charm. I have always found there is plenty of life in such places, but I don't know why on earth I decided to walk that way on this particular night. Anyway, I passed the church and the graveyard, and I had no problems at all. I carried on up the lane. But as I came to the brow of the hill, I began to feel very uneasy. The hairs on the back of my neck stood up, and the further I walked, the more unsettled I became. I started to think there might be someone hiding in the hedge that ran alongside the lane for the whole of its length. But no… it didn't feel quite like that.

As I looked further up the hill, I saw a huge tree at a bend in the lane. And fifteen or twenty feet up the tree I saw two bright flames of light, but I didn't take too much notice of them, because, as I always tell myself, the countryside is full of odd things that usually have a logical explanation. I breathed a sigh of relief, thinking that two owls must be sitting on a branch of the tree, with the headlights from cars passing in the distance reflecting off their eyes.

When I got to about ten feet away from the tree, I stopped and froze. I saw an almighty shadow in front of me, which was thin, but had the shape of a body. It was sort of solid, but not properly solid, and I felt an all-consuming sense of evil.

Whatever this thing was, it knew that I was scared senseless of it. It came towards me. Even if I had been offered all the gold in England, I still wouldn't have been able to move. I screamed out, "Jesus! Help me!" The thing stopped.

I don't know whether it stopped at the sound of my scream, or on hearing the name Jesus, but in that split second, I felt a grain of courage. It was a very tiny grain of courage, I can tell you. I knew that if I turned and ran I would be lost, so I stood my ground, although more out of terror than bravery. I was trembling all over, but somehow I moved, and as I did so, the thing stepped backwards and away from me. I took another step forward, never taking my eyes off it.

As I sidled past this thing, it looked to me like how I imagined pure evil to be. I really thought I was looking at Satan. I saw the most hideous face with grossly distorted features – they were like something you might expect to see in film about aliens. Its eyes had no pupils; they were just like the flames of a fire.

Once I had got round the corner I think I must have broken the four-minute mile. I was shaking for days.

My guides never gave me an explanation about what I had seen that night. About ten years later I was describing the experience to a friend who deals with the paranormal, and he told me it sounded as though I had seen Mothman, a being seen only a few times in history. I told him I had no wish to see it again.

Some time later I left the school for a less demanding career that would allow me more time to work with Spirit. That was the theory, but by now I was known as the 'spirit man', and people came to see me on every conceivable subject.

A Haunting

This phase of my life, which I had thought would be less demanding, brought me plenty of challenges. Reassuring the bereaved that their loved ones carry on was a major part of my work, and yet when I was struck by bereavement myself, it was the most difficult thing on a personal level that I had ever had to deal with.

Another part of my work was travelling to different parts of the country to deal with hauntings. I have had many requests in my life from people to sort out hauntings, though I have to say that in my experience, real hauntings are few and far between. Usually I have found a rational and logical explanation, and the cause of the supposed haunting has been some natural earthly phenomenon. However there have been occasions with no rational explanation.

I once travelled to Yorkshire to try and help a lady who was having problems with a house she had just bought. She was hearing screams in the house, she could hear footsteps going up and down the stairs, and objects were being moved.

When I arrived at the address, my first thought was that the outside of the house wouldn't look out of place in a Jack the Ripper movie. The inside was no better, either. Furniture and boxes were stacked everywhere, and the whole house had a very depressing feel to it. The lady herself, though, was a very practical sort of person, and she was eager for me to start looking round the house.

I made all the usual checks, such as asking how long the house had stood empty and unheated; the old woodwork would be warming up and starting to creak now that the heating was on. I checked upstairs, but I couldn't find anything there apart from an air of depression, which I put down to the fact that there were things stacked everywhere. I couldn't find anything downstairs, either, but I did sense the presence of something bad, and I have learned to trust in my feelings. I was quite puzzled, and I told the lady I would need more time to sort it out. But then she told me the house had a cellar, too, which she intended converting into a kitchen.

A feeling of deep sadness hit me as soon as I opened the cellar door. I also felt very afraid, even though I didn't usually in situations like this. I went down the cellar steps feeling very unsure of myself. Luckily there was a window down there to let in some light, but everything else about the place was horrendous. Things were strewn everywhere, it was damp, and there was water running down a wall from a broken pipe. It felt like someone was there, but I couldn't see anyone yet.

As I moved further into the cellar I heard a rustling sound in the far corner. Then the next thing I knew, something hit me square in the chest. It was a cardboard box, and it was full of paper that spilt out all around me. As I jumped backwards I saw a figure cowering in the corner; it was a young man of about twenty-five. He looked very timid, and he seemed to be terrified of me. After a minute or so I regained my composure, and I said, "Hello, son. Don't be afraid. I only want to talk to you and help you."

I realised I had been wrong about the timid bit, because suddenly he let fly at me with boxes, books and anything else that came to hand. I'm sure I looked like a pile of junk by the time he'd finished, but I wasn't afraid. I knew that he was more afraid of me than I was of him. I took a step forward, but to my horror, he picked up a toilet bowl and threw it at me. I dodged it, and it hit a back wall.

By now I was getting very worried about the lady of the house – she must have thought that World War III had broken out. But I have always told people never to enter when I am working, no matter what the situation. Thankfully, she didn't. Then I spoke again to the young man, saying, "God bless you, son." At this he seemed to crumple, his face a picture of misery.

"I'm afraid," he said. "Don't make me leave. I've nowhere else to go. I've lived here for years, and now that woman has come. I don't like her being here."

After about twenty minutes of talking with him, I was able to show him that there was indeed a place for him. He told me that over the time other people had come to him who had lights around them, but he had been too scared to go with them.

Chou, my guide, then came and took the young man to a place where his family were, and other people he knew. Since then, he has come back to see me, and he is a picture of happiness now. So often I am reminded of the saying 'hope springs eternal' – every time I come across a cause that seems lost.

Rescued

As I have said, in many ways these were strange years for me, but they were happy years, too, for more and more I was seeing the spirit world in all its amazing diversity. In fact I was seeing so many miraculous things that you would never see on earth, that I sometimes couldn't help wondering if I was on my way to living in the spirit world for good.

At this time in my life I was seeing between 150 and 200 people a week, for one reason or another. I was doing a full-time job and looking after a family. I was also travelling a lot, and my health began to suffer. My guides implored me to cut back, but so many people relied on me, and I believed – perhaps arrogantly – that because I was working for the spirit world, I would come to no harm. I was out Christmas shopping one day, when I suffered a mild heart attack.

I was rushed to hospital, and I was told I would be in over Christmas. My reaction to that was to get up two hours later and leave the hospital – with my shopping, I might add. No way were my family going to have their Christmas ruined. I went back home and said nothing. And I would have kept up my silence, but the family doctor turned up on the doorstep, so I had some explaining to do!

My diary was so full at this stage that some of my trips were being booked a year ahead. I had a trip planned for the New Year, and I felt I couldn't let down the people down, so off I went down to London. I was lent a lovely flat to use during my stay.

I took all the meetings and gave all the talks to the various groups as planned, and at the end of the day I returned to the flat. But I was starting to feel unwell.

There was no one else in the flat – well, no one human, anyway. I lay down on the bed, but the next thing I knew, night had fallen, and I felt terribly cold. I could barely move a muscle, and I thought I must have had a stroke. No one would be able to get to me, I thought. I was lying there, feeling sad that my family would fret at the circumstances of my death, when through the open bedroom door I saw a flickering, as if from a fire. I quite expected the living room to be in flames. But to my amazement, a fire had started in the grate, and it was roaring away by now.

I crawled to the hearth and lay there feeling the warmth, knowing that once again I had been saved by the spirit world.

Since that time I have tried a little harder to pace myself, but I find this a very difficult thing to do, because everywhere I go there is someone who needs help from Spirit.

The Rollright Stones

By now I was running a group for people aged between about sixteen and thirty who were interested in the spirit world. Part of the training I gave them took place on field trips to historical sites – I expect this stemmed from the schoolmaster in me.

One day we headed for a place in the Cotswolds called the Rollright Stones, but to my surprise we got lost. We were about to pass by a little country lane when Chou suddenly said, "Turn down here." We turned, and found ourselves driving down a farm track. On the right-hand side stood two very old cottages. I decided I would get out of the car and ask for directions, as Chou was not forthcoming with any further information.

Out of one the cottages came a very elderly lady, who said we were only about a mile from the stones.

"But don't go there," she told us. "That's where they burned the witches who used to live right here." I saw she was pointing to the other cottage, which was derelict.

We found the stones, and we got out of the car to have our picnic. But as we sat and ate, Chou asked me to go into the circle of stones and perform a strange ritual. I performed the ritual, even though Chou had never made such a request in all the years I had known him, and I am not a ritualistic kind of person.

After we had had our lunch, pens and paper were handed around, as there were practical as well as spiritual tasks to achieve. I asked the students to go into the circle and see what their thoughts were and what they could feel, and to write this all down. They took an hour or so doing this, then they sat down and had a cup of tea.

Chou now told me to perform another ritual inside the circle of stones. I told the students that under no circumstances must they come into the circle until I had come out of it.

I felt quite foolish as I complied with Chou's instructions. It seemed to be some kind of cleansing ritual, but it was a lot stranger. As I performed it I could see horse riders, soldiers from times past, and all sorts of different people appearing in the sky around the circle. I finished, left the circle of stones, and rejoined the group.

About ten minutes later a car pulled up and a man and a woman got out. They went into the middle of the circle, and to the amazement of all of us, the man started performing the exact same strange ritual that I had just performed. Some of the group even remarked how similar to me the man looked, but he was certainly a much younger version. At the far side of the circle I could see crowds of people appearing, as if they were preparing for war. Once again Chou told me to enter the circle, stressing that under no circumstances were any of the group to do the same. I relayed Chou's instructions. The students were all very concerned for me, but orders are orders, and I trusted Chou with my life, and always will.

So I entered the circle, and the young man spun round to face me. I was startled to see that his face was full of hate, because as far as I knew, he was a complete stranger to me. I stood my ground as he began circling around me. Out of the corner of my eye I could see the woman starting to do the same. Something akin to anger got the better of me, and this upset me, because I am not prone to anger – people always say I'm so laid back that it's a wonder I don't fall over. I stepped towards the man, ready to do battle, but he ran to the far side of the circle of stones. He stopped and yelled at me: "We've found you now, and you will be destroyed!" Then he and the woman ran to their car. I chased after them, and the group of students ran to catch up with me, but as I got to the car, the man opened the car boot and pulled out a shotgun. I stopped in my tracks, feeling not so brave now. Just then the group arrived, and the man slammed the car boot shut. He jumped into the car, and shouted out the window, "We will destroy your King Stone! This day your armies win, but we will be back."

Well I tried not to show how shaken I was, and we went into a field opposite the Rollright Stones. There we found a huge stone that bore the inscription King Stone. I didn't know what to make of it all. There was no further information from my guides. All they said was, "Well done. The battle starts."

Three weeks later, on a Sunday afternoon, I returned to the Rollright Stones. The recent events had got to me, and my stubborn nature needed to know more.

Nothing happened until I was about to leave the stones, when a large, very expensive-looking car pulled up. Out got a tall, well-built Oriental man, who was aged about 25 and very smartly dressed. He stared at me, and I felt very uncomfortable as I realised his eyes were pure black – they seemed to have no irises. He spoke perfect English, and was very refined, like someone born with a plum in their mouth.

"We know where you are. I am the one who will win this battle, not you or yours."

He turned and drove off, leaving me with my mouth open. What battle, I thought. What on earth was he talking about?

I told my guides that I wanted some answers now, please, as I was starting to feel like I was losing my marbles. I felt like I was in a dream, or a nightmare, to be more accurate... I couldn't believe this was really happening.

Titus spoke up. "You are the link with good, ridding the area of bad forces and all that they are doing. These demon-worshippers see you as a threat to their right to worship evil. But be strong, Joseph, we are with you."

Some comfort, I thought. What if someone comes

at me with a shotgun?

Needless to say, there was a great battle, but I came to no harm in it. I was there, but more as an observer than a participant, in a battle that was essentially being played out in the spirit world. I feel surreal writing about what happened next, but please bear with me.

I sat down near a stone that had a hole in it. A few moments later I heard a very loud gushing sound, like a great wind. It was not a normal kind of wind, though, for the trees were not swaying. The air pressure around me grew extremely heavy.

I wasn't afraid, but I felt a sense of unease when I saw a column of light forming in the middle of the circle of stones. There was a dark shape on the left of this column, which appeared to be some kind of wall. It may not actually have been a wall, but this is the best that I can describe it. Without having been told by anyone, I somehow understood that these were defensive positions, and the battle was about to begin.

Suddenly what I can only describe as a great angel appeared, and then I saw something that I never expected to see in this life or the next, that I wouldn't have missed for the world. The power of good always prevails.

With the World in Her Hands

One night I was sitting at home writing, when I became aware of a great stillness around me. I looked up and saw that my three cats were sitting bolt upright, just staring at an armchair in the corner of the room. Even Mr Wonky Ear had not fled! I looked over towards the chair and I nearly fell off mine in amazement, for sitting in the corner was the most beautiful young lady, surrounded by a wonderful blue and white light. Her white-blonde hair hung long over her shoulders, and she had the clearest of blue eyes. Her dress, from neck to floor, was in blue and silver. And in her hands she held an orb. On looking harder, I realised it was a globe of the world.

I was surprised at the deep voice that came from such a gentle-looking young lady. She said that soon the East and the West would be in conflict, but that peace would come in the form of a child. She said many, many things that night. I could not say how long she stayed, but I wished it would go on forever, so beautiful was her demeanour. I asked her name, but she said, "In time you will know, for in the year 2008 I shall appear to two children. During their lives they shall bring peace where governments cannot." I wait with bated breath for the fulfilment of her prophecy, and also to know who she is.

She smiled at the cats, and said the little one would soon be playing in the spirit world, but I would know she would be well loved and looked after. About three months later my little cat passed into the next life.

The Voice and the People

At this time in my life I felt I should be doing something more constructive for the spirit world. I felt I wasn't really doing anything of true value. Yes, I was receiving accolades of all kinds, and yes, I was seeing hundreds of people, giving readings and talks, and taking meetings. But deep down I felt I was wasting valuable time, and not doing real justice to the knowledge I had been acquiring over the years. In many ways I was longing for the early days, when the spirit world first visited me. Back then it was strange, and I was sometimes very scared, but at least I was working for the spirit world in greater depth.

Then one night that I remember so well, I felt a great sense of peace come over me while I was saying my prayers, and I started to feel a little disoriented. I felt the way you do when you've been to the dentist and been given gas. The room seemed to pulsate in a very gentle way, and I was aware of thousands of tiny flashing lights, of every hue. It was in the centre of the room, as far as I could make out, that a very bright light formed a circle. The circle was about the size of a large plate. I could see a very light bluish-green colour appearing, and through this, I heard the voice of the most powerful energy. I must say, I felt no fear. These were its words:

"The world is in a very sad state. The cries and the prayers of all the people are heard. I shall send to you people from all walks of life and from many nations. You do not need to seek them, for they shall seek you. Be ready, for they will cause you much stress, and even bring you to desperation of mind and soul. There shall be doubters and dissenters, with no faith in themselves. And there shall be others who will live for Spirit, and bring you great joy and happiness. Teach them the ways of true love; teach them the wisdom of hope and faith, so that their truth will be multiplied in all the work they do. Theirs is a special work, for all people of your world. For when the great darkness comes, they will be prepared to bring back the light.

Your leaders walk in dark depths of their own

will, and are feeding the people tares and false hope. So toil on. Your duty is to be a teacher to these workers, and to be like a father to them. Always show goodwill – never show anger, only love, as you have been shown."

"How will I know who these people are?" I asked. "I already see people from all walks of life and from many nations."

The spirit replied, "They will know you, and you will see them by their commitment. They have come again, to fulfil the prophecies of old and new."

"When will all these things come to pass?" I asked.

"The time started when people like yourself came back into your world. These things were spoken to you when you were young."

The spirit was reminding me of the words that Paul had spoken to me when I was a child.

"You will fly to the island of the catacombs, where the saints lived, and you will see the statue of the saint turn to gold, and you will be in great pain," the voice said.

The next thing I knew I had come back to my normal state, but I felt all my skin tingling, as if I'd just had a very hot bath. I had no conception of how much time had passed.

When laid with such heavy responsibilities, I become more aware of my own frailties, and I want to run away and hide – just like other people who do the same sort of work as me must, I feel sure. It is a mixture of my own insecurities and the fear of failure…

In truth I don't always feel calm and loving. How can I speak calmly of all the terrible things that are happening in the world now? I know how Spirit would deal with all these dreadful events, but I wonder whether expressing things in their way is something that my world is ready to accept…

I wrote down everything that happened that night, but weeks turned to months, and no one turned up for me to do the clever things I was expected to do. There was much happening in the family, so the visitation went to the back of my mind.

However the following January, a very cheap package holiday to Malta was available, and I agreed to go, even though I detest flying. We travelled up to Manchester by train and stayed in a hotel overnight, then went on to the airport the next morning.

I was in a state about flying, and was trying to do everything I could think of to calm my nerves. But just my luck, I had to sit next to a lady who didn't stop talking right throughout the flight, and who barely let up drinking. We were crammed in like sardines, and I wasn't enjoying myself at all.

We arrived in Malta, and we were taken from the airport by coach to a place called St Julian's, only to find that our apartment had been double-booked.

Oh, great… I thought. I was being very negative, and even Chou said, "Stop being such a misery! I'm here to enjoy myself. It's not all about you, Joseph."

I felt that even my guide was winding me up! But then the agent said that they had another apartment for us. To my surprise it was huge, and it cost the same as the one-bedroomed apartment we had booked. So I started to cheer up, and even more so later when we went out and I discovered how cheap the drinks were. The days passed, and I really enjoyed myself.

One day we went on a trip to St Paul's Bay, where we found some catacombs. Inside, in white stone, were statues of St Peter and St Paul. I had a Polaroid camera with me, so I took a photograph and waited the allotted time for it to develop.

St Paul came out fine, just as expected, but St Peter had turned a gold colour, and everything in the background behind him had disappeared. I thought the camera was playing up, so I took another photo, this time just of St Peter. This time he was an even brighter gold on an even darker background. Then I photographed St Paul. The white stone of the statue came out perfectly, and the background appeared as normal.

I got talking to the man who looks after the catacombs, and he said that legend has it that St Paul and St Peter lived in the caves for some time.

Once I got outside the catacombs, it hit me! The prophecy that the voice had made all that time earlier was coming to pass. One part of the prediction wasn't, though, because I wasn't in pain.

You would think that by now, after so many years of working with Spirit, I would just accept what I was told…

Two days before returning home, I fell ill with the most incredible pains in my chest. I just wanted to die, but all Chou said was, "See, we told you." I didn't feel that was much help, especially since after I returned home I made countless visits to doctors and hospitals, but I still had the pain for two years, in greater or lesser degrees. Medical experts debated the cause of it, and all Chou kept saying to me was, "No worry, not life-threatening."

True to the word of the voice, people did come to see me. They came from all walks of life and from all over the world. This was a miracle in itself as far as I was concerned, for just as the voice had said, I did not have to go out and seek them, but rather they sought me. Some stayed for a long time; others for shorter periods.

One young man found me after he had dreamed about a man who lived in the city that he had come to study in. His dream kept recurring, so one day he told a friend about it. By chance this friend had come to see me some months earlier. The friend suggested that the young man visit me, in the hope that I might be able to interpret his dream for him. But the moment the young man saw me, he had no need of an interpretation, for he knew that I was the one he had seen in his dream.

Another was a young Indian man. His heart was pure kindness and goodness, and I loved him as if he were my own son.

There is also a young man who speaks many languages. To me he is the heart of everything that promotes goodness to life. Without him these books would not be possible, nor the quality of life that I enjoy.

There are others whom I do not yet mention, because it is their wish that I should not.

I must admit that it is just as well I trust Spirit, for many who came to me tried my patience beyond the endurance of angels, but many others brought me great joy. Mine is not to reason, just to do. I can honestly say that I loved them all. Their task is ahead of them.